Introduct

L **ying** to the west of Wrexham and nort̶ historic upland landscape, with heathe̶ its centre. It is now part of the new *Cl Area of Outstanding Natural Beauty.* On its from World's End is one of the most spectacular limestone escarpments in Britain. Further north is Cyrn-y-Brain with its prominent telecommunication masts. Its northern side includes Llandegla Forest, Esclusham and Minera Mountains, bordered by the Clywedog valley, Minera, Gwynfryn, Bwlchgwyn and Coedpoeth. To the east the moorland extends towards Rhos and Penycae, becoming undulating farmland.

From Minera Lead Mines Visitor Centre and Country Park, the waymarked Clywedog Valley Trail runs east via Bersham Ironworks to the National Trust's Erddig Country Park at the outskirts of Wrexham. Extending north east from Bwlchgwyn is the wooded Nant y Ffrith valley and attractive upland pasture leading to Llanfynydd, Waun-y-Llyn Country Park and Hope Mountain overlooking Caergwrle, with its ancient castle.

This diverse area of upland and valleys has been shaped by man since prehistoric times. Its considerable mineral wealth has been exploited since the Romans, with lead mining, limestone quarrying, coal mining and iron-making playing an important role in the industrial development of north-east Wales. The more rugged moorland of Ruabon Mountain, managed for sheep grazing and later grouse shooting, is complemented by undulating pastureland, wooded valleys, forest, reservoirs and estate land at Erddig. Together they provide a fascinating area to explore.

The 28 walks in this book, which range from an easy 1¼ mile stroll around an upland country park to an exhilarating 10 mile walk exploring the dramatic limestone escarpment of Eglwyseg Mountain, are well within the capability of most people. Many routes contain shorter walk options. A key feature is that individual walks can easily be linked with others to provide longer and more challenging day walks if required. They follow public rights of way or permissive paths, and cross Open Access land. They incorporate sections of the Clywedog Valley Trail, Offa's Dyke Path, and Wat's Dyke. Walking boots are recommended, along with appropriate clothing to protect against the elements. Please remember that the condition of the paths can vary according to season and weather! Contact the relevant local Highways Department regarding any problems encountered (see page 40 for details).

Each walk has a detailed map and description which enables the route to be followed without difficulty, but be aware that changes in detail can occur at any time. The location of each walk is shown on the back cover and a summary of each is provided. This includes an estimated walking time, but allow more time to enjoy the scenery. Many walks are accessible by local bus services.

Please observe the country code and respect any ancient site visited. *Enjoy your walking!*

WAT'S DYKE

DESCRIPTION A 4 mile (**A**) or 2½ mile (**B**) walk exploring the attractive countryside between Caergwrle and Hope, featuring riverside walking, a section of Wat's Dyke and a 17thC packhorse bridge. Allow about 3 hours.
START Caergwrle car park [SJ 305574]
DIRECTIONS The car park adjoins the A541 in the centre of Caergwrle.

W at's Dyke consisted of a 2 metre high bank, with V-shaped ditch to the west. The earthwork ran from Basingwerk, Holywell for 40 miles to Shropshire. Its purpose and exact date is uncertain, but may well pre-date 8thC Offa's Dyke.

I Cross the main road and turn LEFT then RIGHT along a side road past the church. At the junction by The Derby Arms turn LEFT. Continue along Derby Road and Maes Alyn, then follow an enclosed path into a field. Follow the path through three fields (kissing gates) then beside the river Alyn. Cross a stone bridge over the river, then follow it through three fields to join a lane. Go under the railway bridge and along Sarn Lane to a T-junction by the Red Lion in Hope. Go along Kiln Lane past the church and houses to Gresford Road. Turn RIGHT along the verge to a small waymarked gate (Wat's Dyke Path). Follow the enclosed path alongside the tree-covered embanked earthwork of Wat's Dyke to a kissing gate, then to a small metal gate. Follow the fenced path to a kissing gate at the wood corner. (For **Walk B** go through it then resume text in point **4**.)

2 For **Walk A** follow a path LEFT up alongside the wood edge. After crossing an access road continue along a field edge to a pair of kissing gates. Follow the path to a kissing gate in the next field's left hand corner by Stone Cottage. Turn RIGHT along the nearby road, then take a signposted bridleway down the access track to Mountain View Farm. At its entrance cross a stile, go along the field edge then across a stiled footbridge on your left. Turn RIGHT along the field edge

to a stile and continue through the next narrow field to a waymarked gap in its left-hand corner. Go along the wooded edge of two fields.

3 In the corner just before a stile turn RIGHT down a path to cross a stiled footbridge. Go past Little Rhyddyn Farm and follow its access track to the road. Take the signposted path opposite. After a stile it rises steadily past buildings. Shortly in trees take its left fork to a nearby stile. The path then descends past woodland to reach the kissing gate met at point **2**. Turn LEFT.

4 Descend to the wooden fence below then to a kissing gate at the entrance to Rhyddyn Farm. Follow its driveway to the road. Go along the no through road opposite (Fellows Lane). After passing over the railway line the road narrows and descends to its end at Riverside Cottage (note the plaque). Cross the delightful packhorse bridge and follow the railed path up to the road by The Derby Arms to join your outward route.

WALK 2

CAERGWRLE CASTLE

DESCRIPTION A 3¾ mile walk featuring Caergwrle castle, Bryn Yorkin manor house, and a scenic upland road, offering good views. Allow about 3 hours.
START Caergwrle car park [SJ 305574]

C aergwrle Castle has a brief but chequered history. It was built by Dafydd ap Gruffud on land given by Edward I in 1277 as reward for supporting his campaign against his brother Prince Llewelyn. In 1282 Dafydd rebelled against the English, then retreated leaving a partly destroyed castle. Edward rebuilt it for his wife Eleanor of Castile, but it was gutted by fire in 1283 and later abandoned.

I Cross the main road and walk RIGHT past shops and over Castle Street. Just before the War Memorial take the path sign-

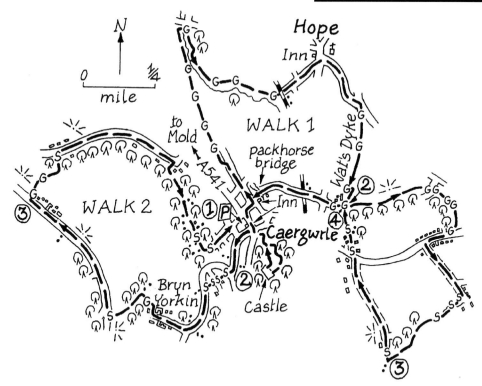

posted to the castle. Follow it through trees up to a path junction. Take the left fork across the slope, then round the wooded edge of the castle mound to enter the ruined castle. Go past the former well, over steps and onto the small ridge ahead. Follow the path down to join your outward route. Cross Wrexham Road then take the narrow lane at the side of Ye Olde Castle Inn to reach Bryn Yorkin Lane. Continue ahead past houses, soon rising.

2 At a junction turn RIGHT along the narrow road then cross a barred stile on the left. Follow the stiled path up to a driveway and on up to rejoin the road. Follow it LEFT, then go up Bryn Yorkin's driveway. Just beyond the Jacobean manor house turn RIGHT past the Malthouse. At its boundary corner bear LEFT to a gate. Angle RIGHT up the path, then just before a stile do a sharp U-turn LEFT and follow the rising path across the wooded slope, then up a field to a stile onto a road. Turn RIGHT up the road, shortly

descending. Continue along the road past Coed Mawr Cottage then Sands Farm.

3 Take a signposted path on the right. Go down the field edge to a gate in the corner into the adjoining field. Go half-LEFT across the steep sloping field to briefly join the boundary opposite, then angle down the slope to a stile in the tree boundary onto a road below by Ochr Farm. Turn RIGHT. The road steadily descends past cottages. On the bend by Celyn Cottage turn RIGHT up a signposted path. At the wall corner turn LEFT and follow the path along the edge of woodland. When it splits go up its right fork to the end of a fence. Ignore the rising path, but follow a less distinct level path by the fence past a small ruin, then a stile on the left. Continue along the woodland edge, soon bending away from the boundary to an iron barred stile. Follow the path past two stiles and on down to a stile on the left. Follow the road down to the car park.

WALK 3
WAUN-Y-LLYN COUNTRY PARK

DESCRIPTION A popular 1¼ mile family walk around a small upland country park offering panoramic views. Allow about 1 hour. A good place to linger.
START Waun-y-Llyn Country Park car park [SJ 286577]
DIRECTIONS From the Railway Inn in Coedtalon on the A5104, turn along Tir y Ffron lane signposted 'Country Park'. Follow the minor road up to a junction. Turn right, then left at the next up to the Park entrance. Also accessible from the A541 north of Caergwrle up a minor road signposted to Horeb.

W *aun-y-Llyn is a small attractive upland Country Park containing a small lake and the remains of a quarry that produced silica sandstone during the 19th and early 20th centuries, which was grounded into silica powder at Coed Talon.*

I Follow a stony path to a kissing gate and on to the high ground ahead above the remains of an old quarry to enjoy all-round views. Follow the path angling RIGHT down the slope and on to cross a raised boardwalk, then two stiles. Follow the path LEFT to pass the side of the lake, then keep to the left fork to cross a stile. Continue with the path across an area of bracken, then a heather-covered rock slab to where you are joined by a path angling in from the left. About 25 yards further, take a path on the left up to a seat at another all-round viewpoint. Now follow a good path south back to the start.

WALK 4
HOPE MOUNTAIN

DESCRIPTION An undulating 5 mile **(A)** or 3½ mile **(B)** walk around Hope Mountain. The route first follows a scenic upland road, then field paths across Hope Mountain. Later it descends and joins a waymarked Flintshire County Council route near Ffrith, which then heads north across wooded quarried slopes, later following a delightful tree-lined bridleway to a road. Here Walk B follows it up to the start. Walk A continues north with the bridleway, then returns through Waen-y-Llyn Country Park. Allow about 3 hours for the full walk. It can easily be undertaken as two separate walks.
START As **Walk 2**.

I Return to the road. Turn LEFT then RIGHT at the junction. Go up the scenic upland road – *enjoying good views from Merseyside to Shropshire*. After ½ mile go through a gate on the right opposite farm buildings and follow an access track to Rhibod. Go past the house to a kissing gate/gate at the end of outbuildings. Just beyond go through a kissing gate on the left. Follow the waymarked path to a stile/gate, then between boundaries to a gate. Cross a stile on the right just beyond. Follow the enclosed narrow green track to a gate then to a road. Follow it LEFT then cross a stile on the right.

2 Follow the fence/tree boundary up the field to go through a gateway in it just before the top corner. Continue up the adjoining field to a green shelf. In the corner turn LEFT down the field edge to a stile. Continue down the next field, over a cross path, to cross the fence into trees (stile requested) on the right about 30 yards before the field corner. Follow the path past a small ruin and down through the trees to cross a stile, then descend the path to the entrance to Rock Cottage Farm. Go down its driveway to a minor road. Follow it RIGHT, then take a signposted path angling off on the left to join a section of a waymarked Flintshire circular

walk. Follow the path through the trees. Shortly, the path emerges into a small clearing and splits. Keep ahead through the clearing, then through trees. It then bends north past a side path and a good viewpoint, after which it rises through the trees to a stile. The path continues across more open ground, then soon angles LEFT down to a fence corner. Follow the waymarked path down to a stile.

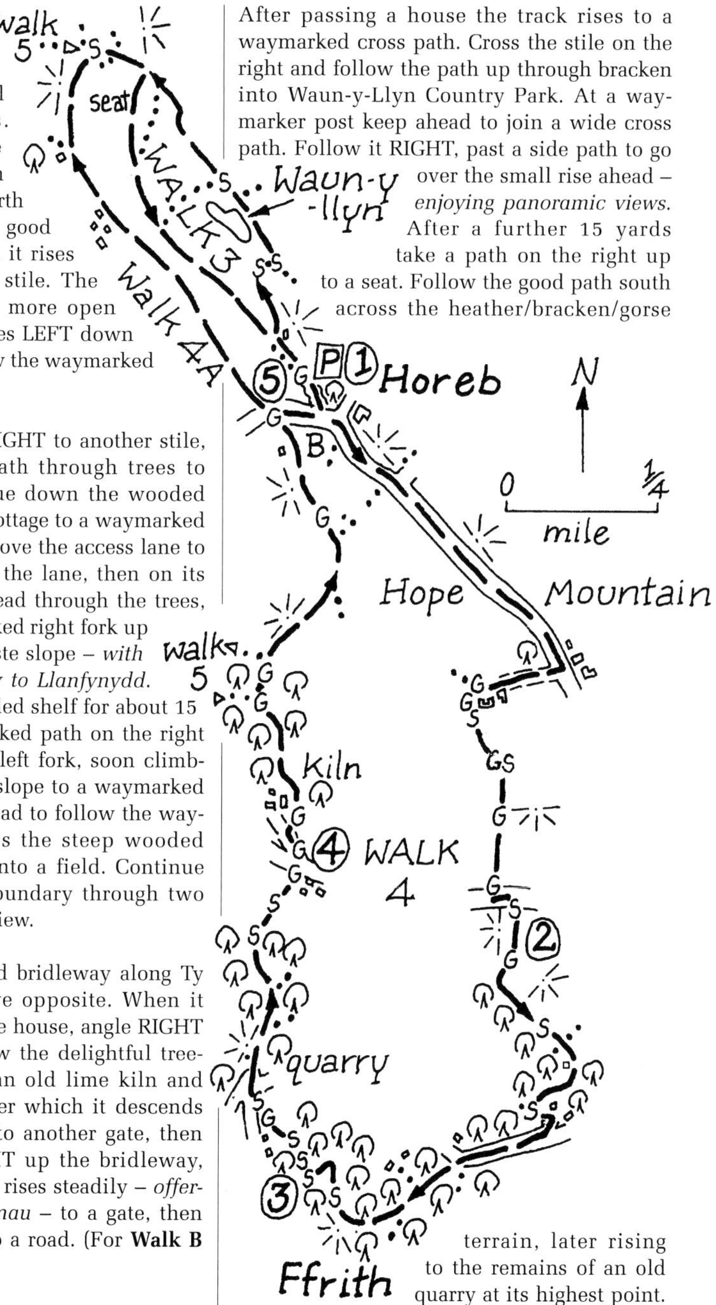

3 Just beyond turn RIGHT to another stile, then follow the path through trees to a further stile. Continue down the wooded slope passing above a cottage to a waymarked wooden gate, and on above the access lane to a stile/steps. Go down the lane, then on its bend, follow a path ahead through the trees, soon taking its waymarked right fork up across a more open waste slope – *with a view along the valley to Llanfynydd.* Go across the part wooded shelf for about 15 yards to take a waymarked path on the right through trees. Take its left fork, soon climbing across the wooded slope to a waymarked path junction. Keep ahead to follow the waymarked path up across the steep wooded slope to a stone stile into a field. Continue ahead alongside the boundary through two fields to a road by Fairview.

4 Take the signposted bridleway along Ty Ucha's access drive opposite. When it bends down towards the house, angle RIGHT to a nearby gate. Follow the delightful tree-lined bridleway, past an old lime kiln and former quarry, soon after which it descends to a gate. Keep ahead to another gate, then just beyond turn RIGHT up the bridleway, soon tree-lined again. It rises steadily – *offering a view of Moel Famau* – to a gate, then continues past a ruin to a road. (For **Walk B** turn right.)

5 Go along the signposted bridleway opposite, soon on a green track. Later it steadily descends, then passes an old farm.

After passing a house the track rises to a waymarked cross path. Cross the stile on the right and follow the path up through bracken into Waun-y-Llyn Country Park. At a waymarker post keep ahead to join a wide cross path. Follow it RIGHT, past a side path to go over the small rise ahead – *enjoying panoramic views.* After a further 15 yards take a path on the right up to a seat. Follow the good path south across the heather/bracken/gorse terrain, later rising to the remains of an old quarry at its highest point. Divert to the left for all-round views, then continue along the stony path to a kissing gate into the car park.

Map labels: walk 5, seat, WALK 3, Walk 4A, Waun-y-Llyn, Horeb, N, mile, 0, ¼, Hope Mountain, walk 5, kiln, WALK 4, quarry, Ffrith

WAUN-Y-LLYN & WOOD PITT

DESCRIPTION A 4¼ mile (**A**) or 4 mile (**B**) walk exploring the attractive countryside between Coed-talon and Llanfynydd. After an initial climb the route passes through Waun-y-Llyn Country Park, with its small lake and panoramic views, then descends the hillside by field paths and a tree lined bridleway. After a choice of routes, including an optional visit to an inn in Llanfynydd, the final section follows a former railway line through Wood Pitt Nature Reserve.

START Car park by the Old Chapel, Coed-talon [SJ] 269589] or Waun-y-Llyn Country Park car park [SJ] 286577]

DIRECTIONS At the Railway Inn on the A5104 as you enter Coed-talon from Pontybodkin, turn along Tir y Ffron lane signposted 'Country Park' to find small car park on the right.

I Follow the road past the old chapel and up to a T-junction by Tri Thy Craft Centre. Continue ahead then take a signposted path over a stile on the right opposite Tir y Paenau. Follow the boundary on the left – *enjoying good open views west from Moel Famau to Llandegla Moors* – round to a stile. Go up the field edge to a stile in the top boundary onto a narrow green track. Follow it LEFT then with a cottage just ahead, do a sharp U-turn to a nearby slate stile/gate to enter Waun-y-Llyn Country Park (See **Walk 3** for information).

2 Follow the path through heather and gorse, past a path on the right, after which it bends left to be joined by a path angling in from the right to go over a small rise – *offering panoramic new views of the Dee estuary, Merseyside, the Lancashire coast, Cheshire and distant Pennines.* The path continues across the bracken, gorse, rowan covered terrain, past a descending path on the right. Just beyond take the path's left fork through gorse, across a heather-covered rock slab and on to a stile. *Ahead can be seen Waun-y-Llyn's rocky summit.* Follow

the path past the lake to cross a stile on your right and another just beyond. Cross a raised boardwalk and follow the path up to the craggy top – *offering all round views.* Follow the stony path to a kissing gate and car park, then a lane to the road.

3 From the entrance to the Country Park turn LEFT, then RIGHT at the nearby junction. Take a signposted path over a stile on the right. Angle LEFT up the field to cross an old low wall corner and down across the next two fields to cross a stile in the far corner to join an enclosed bridleway. Follow it LEFT down between tree-lined boundaries. At the bottom you have a choice. (For **Walk B** cross the waymarked stile ahead above outbuildings. Follow the path down through trees to cross two stiles then continue with the tree-lined sunken path to a stile/gate. Follow the access track to the road. Follow it to the B5101 at point **5**.)

4 For **Walk A** follow the bridleway LEFT to go through a nearby waymarked gate. Follow the bridleway through the trees, then at another gate cross a stile on the right. Descend through trees to cross a stile on the left. Continue down the edge of the long field, then angle LEFT to a stile near the bottom corner. Follow the tree boundary on your right to cross a stile in it midway along the field. Angle LEFT down the field to a gate in the corner. (This gives access to a road which you can follow to the Cross Foxes in Llanfynydd for refreshments then continue through the village to rejoin the main route at point **5**.) Here turn RIGHT along the field edge past a house to cross a stile in the corner and one beyond. Follow the stiled path across two further fields to reach the road, where you are joined by Walk B. Follow it LEFT to the B5101 at the outskirts of Llanfynydd. Turn RIGHT.

5 Follow the road with care to an information board at the entrance to Wood Pitt Nature Reserve. Now follow the tree-lined bridleway along the former railway line past Coed Talon marsh to the start. *This marshy valley was once a thriving industrial area, for adjoining the line were Wood Pitt and*

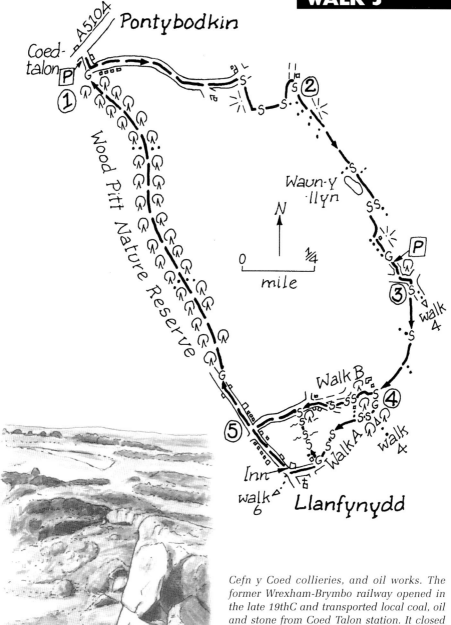

Pontybodkin

Coed-talon

Wood Pitt Nature Reserve

Waun-y-llyn

N

0 ———— ¼
mile

walk 4

Walk B

Walk A

walk 4

Inn

walk 6

Llanfynydd

Cefn y Coed collieries, and oil works. The former Wrexham-Brymbo railway opened in the late 19thC and transported local coal, oil and stone from Coed Talon station. It closed in the 1950s, but in 2004 this section was opened as a recreational route.

Waun-y-llyn Country Park

7

WALK 6

NANT Y FFRITH I

DESCRIPTION A 5 mile walk exploring the varied undulating countryside between Llanfynydd, Ffrith and Bwlchgwyn, including the wooded Nant y Ffrith valley, with traditional inns on route. Allow about 3 hours.
START Llanfynydd [SJ 279567] or Bwlchgwyn War Memorial [SJ 263536]
DIRECTIONS Llanfynydd lies on the B5101. See **Walk 7** for the alternative start.

*From the 18th-20thC the valley between Llanfynydd and Ffrith saw extensive quarrying and mining for coal, silica, limestone, sandstone, as evidenced by shafts, limekilns, quarries, tramways and railways. Whilst both villages grew during the boom years of the late 19th/early 20thC, artefacts found and archaeological evidence indicates that Ffrith was originally a Roman settlement. The villages are connected by the B5101 road which follows the line of Offa's Dyke, and by the former Brymbo – Coedtalon mineral railway line. Ffrith stands on an important 17/18thC pack-horse route and a stone pack-horse bridge can still be seen. For information on Nant y Ffrith see **Walk 7**.*

1 From Llanfynydd take a signposted path along a track opposite the car park of the Cross Foxes and behind the PO/stores. It passes under a small iron footbridge. When it splits continue ahead to pass between Mill House and a garage to a stile beyond. *Nearby is the former stone Corn Mill.* Continue to cross a footbridge over the steam and a stile from which run two waymarked paths. Follow the path directly ahead across the field to a stile in the tree boundary.

2 Follow the path across the lower slopes to a stile/gate onto a road. Take a signposted path along the track opposite to Rhewl farm. Pass between buildings and the end of the house to go through a waymarked gate. Go along the left-hand edge of the field to a stile/gate and another just beyond to join an access track opposite Glandwr. Turn

LEFT down a rough tree-lined track to pass under the former mineral railway, then cross a stile by a gate on the right. Follow the green track running below the old railway, soon passing beneath large lime kilns. The track continues through a field to a stile/gate, then past industrial buildings – *where nearby two Roman kilns were found* – and the Blue Bell Inn to reach an information board by the main road in Ffrith. (*A short walk along Cymau Road opposite brings you to the old pack-horse bridge and ford.*)

3 Here do a sharp U-turn to go along the adjoining Valley Road past houses and under the old railway viaduct. Go straight ahead on a signposted path along the middle of three tracks. Follow it past Pant Isa farm to its end just before a large extended house. Here turn LEFT on the signposted path (Bwlchgwyn) and follow the fenced path passing below the end of the house and on through trees to a small gate. Now follow the path – *a former estate road* – through the Nant y Ffrith valley, later passing an open view across the wooded valley. Go past a cross-path and just beyond a green track on the right you meet two narrow tracks. Ignore the one with a kissing gate/gate (unless returning to Bwlchgwyn), but bear RIGHT along the ungated track, which rises steadily to emerge from the trees onto the bend of a stony forestry track.

4 Turn RIGHT then take a path from nearby swings – *an unexpected sight* – back into the wood. Follow this wide walled stony path – *a former estate road* – past a small ruin and across a clearing to re-enter the wood. Here the path splits by an old stile. Continue ahead on the wide stony path, rising steadily through the mixed woodland. Shortly angle RIGHT across a forestry track and continue up the wide path opposite. Later the path suddenly narrows and splits. Ignore its rising left fork and take the more indistinct level right fork through an attractive area of birch, rowan, heather & bilberry to a stile at the edge of the wood – *offering extensive views of the Dee estuary, Merseyside, Hope Mountain, Cheshire and distant Pennines.* Follow the path across reedy upland pasture to a stile, then along the next field edge – *enjoying new views west to Moel Famau* – shortly descending, then bending away from a small wood. It then does a U-turn above a small bricked building and passes through a section of the wood to a stile/gate by two other small buildings. The path now descends to a gate onto a road.

5 Continue along the road ahead and just before the entrance to Gwlfa cross a stone stile by a gate on the left. Go ahead along the edge of two fields, then follow the hedge on your right through two further fields to Pentre farm. Go past the farm buildings to

the road. Turn LEFT then after a few yards RIGHT to cross a stile and another just out of sight. After a third stile bear LEFT down the field to a stile in the fence, then continue down the next field towards Llanfynydd to cross a stile in the right-hand corner. Turn RIGHT along the field edge and on down to a stile/gate ahead onto the bend of a road. Turn LEFT along a green track, then just before a gate, turn RIGHT on a path through trees to a stile. Follow the tree boundary on your left for about 15 yards then angle RIGHT down the slope to join your outward route at the stile below. (If you started from Bwlchgwyn, just before the stile below, turn sharp right and resume text at paragraph **2**.)

Alternative start from Bwlchgwyn: Follow instructions in paragraph **1** of **Walk 7**, then turn right up the narrow track to a kissing gate/gate, where you join the main route. Turn sharp left along another track up to the bend of a stony forestry track at point **4**.

WALK 7

NANT Y FFRITH 2

DESCRIPTION A 5 mile walk from Bwlchgwyn through the wooded Nant y Ffrith valley to the Roman settlement of Ffrith, later a thriving industrial village, offering a choice of inns. The walk returns by an old pack-horse trail, quiet lanes and field paths. Allow about 3 hours.
START Bwlchgwyn War Memorial [SJ 263536]
DIRECTIONS At the northern end of Bwlchgwyn on the bend of the A525 is a parking area on the right by the war memorial and information boards – offering good views towards Shropshire and north to Moel Famau.

*N**ant y Ffrith valley**, now densely wooded and tranquil, was once a thriving industrial area. Lead has been mined here since Roman times, with the last mine closing in 1857. Quarries provided building stone which was carried away by tramways. During the mid-19thC a fine country estate was established in the then more open valley, developing through various owners into a 24 bedroomed Hall, exotic gardens, tennis courts and stables. In the 20thC the estate steadily deteriorated and during the Second World War the Hall was used as a munitions store and then demolished. Apart from the stables and some exotic trees among the pines, nothing remains of this grand country house. The woods are now owned and managed by Borderlands Forestry. (For information on Ffrith see **Walk 6**.)*

1 Go down the nearby minor road (Glascoed Road) past houses, then take a signposted path on the left at the end of a small wood. When it splits keep ahead to descend past a small quarry to a lane. Cross the stile opposite and follow the path down through mature mixed woodland, over a track, and down through further trees to another track. Follow it LEFT across a bridge over the river.

2 Turn LEFT along the track. Just before the gated entrance of the former stables take the waymarked path past its right hand

side, then up through trees, later levelling out to go through a bridle gate onto a lane. Turn RIGHT and follow the signposted path to gates ahead by information boards. Go up the stony forestry track, soon bending right. When it bends sharp left head to nearby swings, from where a path enters the wood. Follow this wide walled stony path – *a former estate road* – past a small ruin and across a small clearing passing under power cables, to re-enter the wood. Here the path splits by an old stile. Go down the path's right fork. At the bottom the waymarked path bends RIGHT, then after a few yards LEFT down to join a nearby wide cross path – *another former estate road*.

3 Follow it LEFT through the wooded valley to eventually reach a small gate, soon after which you emerge into the open. The path now bends right passing below a nearby large house. Go down its access track, past Nant Isa farm, to eventually reach the old railway viaduct at Ffrith. *This is the former Brymbo-Coed-talon mineral line which carried material from the quarries. For refreshments go along the road to the Bluebell Inn or the Poachers.*

4 Turn sharp RIGHT to cross the river, then bear RIGHT to join the old pack-horse trail, now a bridleway, above the river. *For generations, especially during the 17th and 18thC, pack-horses made regular trips through the hills carrying goods for selling at markets in England, and returning with other goods. This particular trail may have been used by the Romans. The delightful tree-lined mossy old trail rises steadily to pass under a small bridge – a disused tramway to a nearby 19th C stone quarry. The bridleway continues up past Glascoed Hall – dating from the 17thC. It then bends left – the original pack-horse trail continued straight ahead – and passes a good viewpoint looking east to Cheshire and the distant Pennines. At the road turn LEFT past Glascoed Cottage and a complex of houses, after which the road bends right above a wooded valley.*

5 Just before the road does a sharp U-turn, take a signposted path on the right across

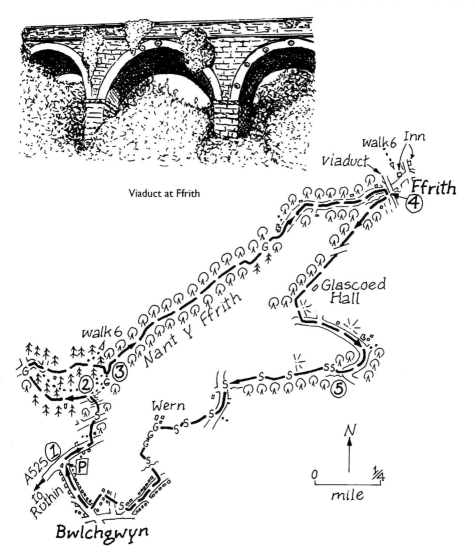

Viaduct at Ffrith

a stream and on up through trees to cross two stiles at the top. Now follow the stiled path along the edge of three fields – *good views looking back* – to a road. Turn LEFT up the road. Shortly take a signposted path over a stile on the right. Angle LEFT across the field to a stile in the corner. Keep ahead to another stile, then up the field to go through two gates by Wern farm. *A 17thC building here was used as a stop for pack-horses travelling between Wales and Chester.* Turn LEFT to go through the left of two facing gates. Follow the fence on your right to a gate then along the next field edge. In the corner turn LEFT to a stile in the next corner. Cross the stream then follow the path up to a road. Follow it RIGHT. Just before the T-junction take a signposted path on the right to a stile. Continue past a graveyard, over an access track, and on with the enclosed path to a house. Turn LEFT along its access track to the main road. Turn RIGHT back to the start.

WALK 8

AROUND MINERA

DESCRIPTION A 4½ mile (**A**), 3 mile (**B**) or 2¼ mile (**C**) walk exploring the attractive countryside and history around the industrial communities of Coedpoeth, Minera and Gwynfryn, with a pub midway. The route meanders along the wooded Clywedog valley to Minera. Walk A continues to Gwynfryn, before returning by a former quarry road, then railway path through Minera Lead Mines Country Park, being joined by the shorter walks. Allow about 3 hours.

START Minera Lead Mines Centre [SJ 276509]

DIRECTIONS At the Five Crosses Inn on the A525 near Coedpoeth take the B5426 signposted to Minera/ Lead Mines. Follow the road through Minera to reach the site after 1¼ mile.

C oedpoeth (*Burnt Wood*) *stands above the Clywedog valley. An area known as 'The Smelt ' was once used for lead smelting, using local trees for charcoal. The village developed with the exploitation of coal, ironstone, lead, zinc and silica. For information on Minera see* **Walk 20**.

I Return to the entrance then take the signposted path opposite (Coedpoeth). Follow the enclosed path down to cross a footbridge over the river then up the wooded slope. Soon take another fenced path on the left back across the wooded slope to join an access track by houses. Follow it RIGHT, then at a finger post continue along the road ahead. Take a signposted path (Minera) along the first road on the left. At its end turn LEFT along the fenced path to a road and entrance to a goods yard. Take the signposted path opposite down through trees then continue along the edge of the wooded valley, shortly descending to the river. Follow the path RIGHT beside the river past a waymarked side path and on through the wooded valley. At a wide descending path by a waymarker post turn LEFT to continue by the river to a footbridge. Here you have a choice. **Option 1:** Cross the footbridge and follow the path

along the river's left bank, soon rising to a track, then descend a path to cross another footbridge. **Option 2:** Continue with a stiled riverside path to another footbridge.

2 Go up the railed path above the stream to a kissing gate and continue ahead past the school to the road in Minera. Cross the road and bear LEFT along Church Road past a telephone box and bus shelter. Continue past Plas Gwyn and a children's playground, then take a signposted path on the left (Pentre). *You may first be tempted by Tyn y Capel just ahead, offering traditional pub food.* Follow the path down into the wooded valley to a footbridge over the river and on to a road. Turn RIGHT. On the bend you have a choice. (For **Walk C** follow the road left up to join the railway path at point **5**.) For **Walk A/B** follow the path signposted to the Lime Works up the track ahead to a kissing gate/gate. Continue along the wide path up the wooded valley to another kissing gate, then past woodland to a small gate to join the railway path. (For **Walk B** follow it LEFT to point **5**.)

3 For **Walk A** follow it RIGHT. Just before a kissing gate with houses beyond, turn RIGHT along another path to a nearby kissing gate. Turn RIGHT along a woodland path – *a former mineral railway line.* After about 100 yards, turn LEFT along a side path past outbuildings and Maes y ffynon cottage to the road. Follow it LEFT then take the signposted path (Ffordd yr Ysgol) on the right. Go past the side of White Cottage to a stile ahead. Follow the tree boundary on your right to another stile. Keep ahead to cross the stream and go up the field beyond to a house, then follow its driveway to the road above at Gwynfryn. Turn LEFT then go along the left fork. At a junction, go up Allt Eistedfod. After passing signposted paths, the road descends. On the bend by a ruin go past a kissing gate to go through another by a gate.

4 Go down the old quarry road, past signposted side paths, to a kissing gate/gate into an expansive area of old quarry. *It pro-*

vided limestone for the Limeworks just down the valley. Established in 1852, at its peak the Limeworks had 17 kilns, its own steam locomotives and wagons, carrying lime and limestone to iron and steel works and chemical manufacturers. It finally closed in 1972 and its railway was dismantled. Stone continued to be extracted from the quarry for road building until it closed in 1992. Follow the old quarry road along the valley past part hidden kilns. After a kissing gate/gate continue along the road, then just before the barrier gate angle RIGHT to a kissing gate between buildings at the entrance to Rock Cottage. Follow the path past houses to go through the right of two kissing gates ahead to join your outward route. Follow the tree-lined railway path past point **3** to a road.

5 Continue along the former Minera branch railway (1851-1972), past Lloyd's Engine House (1860), then the site of Taylor's Shaft to cross a road by a nearby junction. Follow the path through the trees, over another road and through a kissing gate opposite. Ignore the tree-lined wide path ahead, but turn LEFT and follow an adjoining path along the top

The Engine House

N

0 — 1/4 mile

wynfryn

of a meadow, then a stony track to pass the restored chimney and Engine House to reach the Visitor Centre – housing an interesting exhibition about the lead mines and providing light refreshments. Just beyond turn LEFT down the pathway to the car park.

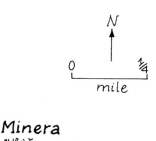

Minera
Inn
School
Coedpoeth
The Smelt
Engine House
Engine House
Taylor's Shaft
Lead Mines Centre
walks 20/21

WALK 9

AROUND MINERA MOUNTAIN

DESCRIPTION A 9 mile walk, of great variety, for experienced walkers. The route first follows the popular railway path through Minera Lead Mines Country Park, then other paths to enter an area of more demanding Open Access moorland. The route heads to an attractive hidden side valley then follows the course of its stream along a more shallow reedy valley to join a minor upland road. The next section follows a path across heather moorland down to Frondeg, then returns by minor roads and field paths. **START** Minera Lead Mines Centre [SJ 276509] **DIRECTIONS** See **Walk 8**.

I Take the pathway behind the Information Board up to a finger post. Turn RIGHT to pass behind the Visitor Centre, then Meadow Engine House and chimney. Continue ahead, soon on a path across the top of a field to a kissing gate. Cross the road and follow the path through the trees to another road and a small gate opposite. Continue along the former Minera branch railway (1851-1972), past the site of Taylor's shaft and the former Lloyd's Engine House (1860). Cross a road then continue along the railway path now signposted to the Lime Works. Follow it for ½ mile to a kissing gate. Go past the first house and outbuilding and continue to a kissing gate between buildings at the entrance to Rock Cottage and the former Lime Works site. Go to a kissing gate/gate ahead then go along the former quarry road to a footbridge across the stream at an expansive limestone quarry. (*See paragraph 4 of Walk 8 for information.*) Continue up to the nearby kissing gate/gate and follow the old quarry road up through trees.

2 Shortly take a signposted path on the left opposite one signposted to Eisteddfod. Follow it up through the part wooded slope to a stile. Turn LEFT – *with a good view over-*

looking the vast quarry – then follow a farm track RIGHT up through bracken – *later with views to Moel Famau, Merseyside, and Cheshire.* When it fades bear LEFT round to a way-marked fence corner, then continue to a stile in the left hand field corner. Follow the waymarked path ahead along the track through Ty Hir farm to a gate at the last building. Follow the track past an old house, bending RIGHT to a stile/gate. Continue along the green track to a stile/gate into open moorland. Follow the old reedy track, then path near the boundary. At its corner keep ahead through reeds to join a good path, which shortly bends LEFT down to cross a stream. After a further 50 yards descend a small bilberry/heather gully into a shallow reedy valley. Go LEFT along it, then turn RIGHT across a wet reedy area and follow a path up to a small wooden post. A few yards beyond as the path heads up to the nearby fence, to avoid beehives angle RIGHT up across the tussocky bilberry/heather terrain to overlook a deeper valley. Angle down the slope to a small fenced shaft then descend to cross the stream.

3 Follow the path RIGHT along the edge of the wide shallow valley by the stream. When it bends left cross it and keep ahead to where you overlook it again. Here angle RIGHT up the slope to continue on an improving path along the right rim of the valley. Shortly the path bends RIGHT towards the distant forest. After about 40 yards descend LEFT across the now exposed side stream. Go up a path opposite. Just after

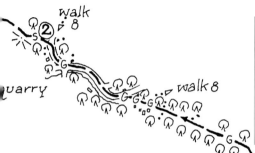

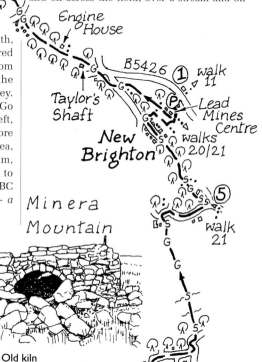

through reeds, then continues down through bracken to a stile/gate. At the next fence corner the path bears LEFT to a stile/gate by a mast and power substation at Fron-deg. Go along the track, then turn RIGHT down the road, past side roads. At a T-junction turn LEFT down the tree-lined road. Just after it bends right take a signposted path (New Brighton) on the left. Go up the slope ahead and on across the field, over a stream and on

it bends left, angle RIGHT along another path, then descend into the main bracken covered valley. Continue along its right hand bottom edge. After crossing the stream twice the path continues along the now wider valley. Just after a post keep to the right fork. Go past a solitary tree a little way to your left, then after about another 50 yards, just before the embankment reaches a large reedy area, descend a path on the left. Cross the stream, then continue to a visible road sign ahead to join the road by a waymarker post and WCBC boundary post. Turn LEFT up the road – *a relief after the moorland terrain.*

4 After 1 mile on its second left bend by a few large stones and a nearby old waste tip turn RIGHT along a green track. Just beyond the tip bear LEFT to ascend a sunken path, soon levelling out – *offering panoramic views* – and reaching a ruined limekiln – *a good place for a break.* Follow a discernible path ahead, keeping to the left of two parallel paths. Follow it south eastwards on a long gentle descent through reedy/heather moorland. After crossing a water channel it bends

to cross a footbridge and stile. Go up the next field edge to a gate and on up to another, then follow the next field edge to a stile. Bear LEFT to the bend of a nearby road by a large house. Turn RIGHT down the road past a farm.

5 Now follow instructions in paragraph **3** of **Walk 21**.

WALK 10

ESCLUSHAM MOUNTAIN

DESCRIPTION A 2¾ mile walk exploring Esclusham Mountain featuring panoramic views and hidden delights amongst the heather moorland. The route makes a short climb up Esclusham Mountain to visit an old mine, then the summit trig point, before descending to the road. On the return it diverts (optional) to visit attractive hidden side valleys. Allow about 2 hours.

START Roadside beneath Esclusham Mountain [SJ 255512].

DIRECTIONS Heading south from Minera on the B5426 take a side road signposted to World's End. Follow it up the hillside for nearly 1 mile to find parking options just beyond a small pool on the right, and a track.

other track, then path, to the summit trig point. Follow the path ahead down through heather, later joined by another path, to spoil heaps. Here turn RIGHT down an old green track to the road. Turn RIGHT down the road.

2 Just before it bends half-right, turn LEFT along a stony track through an area of old workings. It soon peters out by a small lilly covered pool. Just beyond take a path angling RIGHT, soon heading towards the far forest corner. It then gently descends past areas of stones and a small low ruin. When the path bears half-right keep ahead to the rim of a valley, with three trees and a small fenced shaft opposite. Descend the small gully, then angle RIGHT down to a path by the stream. Follow it RIGHT. Soon turn RIGHT up a delightful side valley (probably dry). Just before scrap metal where the stream shows on the surface, follow a path LEFT up the slope. Soon bear RIGHT through the right hand side of a clearing amongst the bracken, then turn RIGHT along a path parallel with the side valley. Cross the stream at the top to rejoin the stony track above and nearby road.

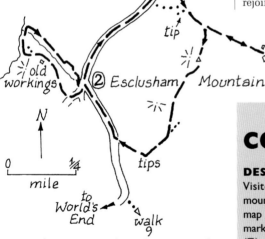

1 Take a green track up the western slope of Esclusham Mountain, past a tip, then a fainter distinct track near the top. Continue along the track to the expansive site of an old mine, with rectangular pools, old buildings and spoil heaps set amongst the heather moorland. Retrace your steps and take the

WALK 11

COED LLANDEGLA

DESCRIPTION Llandegla Forest, with its Visitor Centre/restaurant offers waymarked mountain bike trails and forest walks (a detailed map is available). I have incorporated the waymarked walks into a choice of 5 mile (**A**), 3 mile (**B**) and 2½ mile (**C**) walks. After visiting a RSPB hide at the forest/moorland edge, which is maintained as a habitat for the rare black grouse, Walk A extends west, while the others visit Pendinas Reservoir. Allow between 2–3 hours.

START Coed Llandegla Visitor Centre [SJ 241523]

DIRECTIONS The Centre is signposted off the A525 between Ruthin and Wrexham. Note car park closing time.

From information boards by the Centre/ restaurant follow the waymarked walks up to and through the higher car park to a gate at its end. After briefly continuing along the stony track, the waymarked path then runs close by it, passing wooden owl sculptures. Later, after passing more through the forest edge the waymarked walks split. Cross the forestry track and follow the purple/Black Grouse walk ahead to reach several large wooden black grouse sculptures at the forest edge. Turn RIGHT along the track. After visiting the hide retrace your steps to follow the nearby purple walk back to the main forestry track. (For **Walk A** follow it LEFT up to a track junction, then follow the track/ brown walk ahead. After nearly a mile turn RIGHT along the Offa's Dyke Path through the trees. At another forestry track turn RIGHT and follow it to a track junction where you join the blue walk. Turn LEFT and follow the track past bike trails, afterwards bending right to go through a gate at point **3**.)

2 For Walks B/C keep ahead on the purple walk, soon descending through the forest to cross a bike trail, then joining the family bike trail near the reservoir. Follow the trail along the embanked end of the reservoir to a path junction at post 14. (For **Walk C** keep ahead past a picnic area and round the edge of the reservoir, passing over the dam. The waymarked walk

then enters the forest, passes a bike trail and rejoins your outward route. Follow it back to the Centre.) For **Walk B** follow the waymarked orange walk LEFT down to a track junction. Turn LEFT.

3 Follow the nearby signposted bridle-way/waymarked walks through the trees, soon descending steadily to cross a stream in the valley bottom. Turn RIGHT, then bend sharp LEFT up a track and follow the undulating track along the forest edge. Later the waymarked walk turns RIGHT off the track, passes through trees and crosses a wide forestry track. It then continues as a stony path to a path junction in a small clearing. Take the right fork to reach a forestry track by large utility buildings. Turn RIGHT up the track, past bike trails, to a gate onto the bend of a track. Angle LEFT down to join your outward path above the Centre.

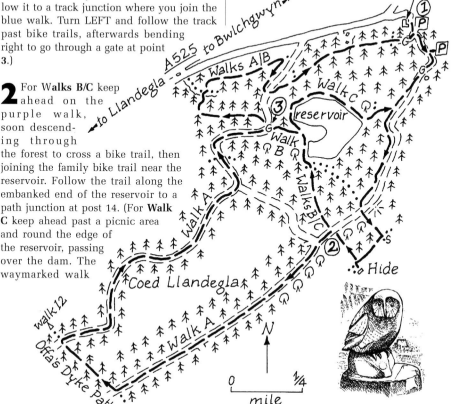

17

WALK 12

CYRN-Y-BRAIN & COED LLANDEGLA

DESCRIPTION A 7 mile walk exploring Open Access moorland, offering panoramic views, and contrasting forest with a café to finish. Starting at just over 1300 feet the route follows a track up to three prominent telecommunication stations on the broad heather top of Cyrn-y-Brain, then visits the trig point and ruins of Sir Watkin's Tower (1847 feet/563 metres). After following Offa's Dyke Path down through Llandegla Forest, the route returns by quiet country road and moorland paths. Allow about 4 hours.

START The Ponderosa Café & Gift Shop, Horseshoe Pass [SJ 193481]

DIRECTIONS The Ponderosa adjoins the A542 at the top of the Horseshoe Pass. There is an informal off-road parking area opposite.

1 Cross the road to the Ponderosa and turn LEFT along the grass verge past the car park. At its corner, angle RIGHT across the side road and follow a path ahead through heather and gorse to a stile/gate on a stony track. Follow the path signposted to Sir Watkin's Tower along the rough track, soon rising steadily towards a transmitter mast. The track then meanders up the heather slopes of Cyrn-y-Brain to eventually level out by the first wireless station and a stone cairn.

2 Continue along the track past another mast, then when it bends to the third mast keep ahead along a green track – *enjoying great views from the Clwydian Range to Shropshire Hills, and west to Snowdonia.* Continue with a path through the heather beside the fence across Cyrn-y-Brain – *enjoying new views east to Cheshire and the Pennines.* After visiting the trig point and the site of Sir Watkin's Tower – *built as a folly by a prominent landowner on a Bronze*

Age cairn in the late 18thC or early 19thC, offering superb views – continue on the signposted link path to Offa's Dyke Path alongside the fence. It gently descends across the expansive moorland towards Coed Llandegla and passes a stile accessing a parallel forestry track (another option). Continue ahead on a narrower path through heather alongside the forest to join the Offa's Dyke Path.

3 Cross the nearby ladder-stile into the forest and follow the stony track to a forestry road. Continue on the Offa's Dyke Path down to another forestry road. The path now descends steadily through the forest past a cycle trail. After a cross path it briefly runs alongside a stream in a small clearing, passes two cycle trails, then continues down through the forest. Soon after crossing another forestry road it leaves Coed Llandegla by a small gate, then continues down past a house to reach a road by Nant-yr-hafod studio. Follow it LEFT past Trefydd-Bychain and through lush farmland grazed by cattle. After passing Graig Farm and houses the road rises steadily, passing through a gate and continuing up beneath the forest.

4 Shortly, take a track angling up on the left. On its bend follow a green track ahead to a gate into Open Access land. Go up the old track, soon bending left up above a side valley. Shortly, take a path on the right to cross the nearby stream by a small rowan tree, and on to a fence corner. Continue alongside the fence. Just before it descends to a stream, turn LEFT for a few yards, cross the stream, then follow a path initially near it, soon passing a small rowan tree then a small holly tree. After an unexpected view of the Ponderosa ahead, the path continues above a side valley to a footbridge over a stream, then heads west. At a slate waymarker post at a path junction, continue ahead (Horseshoe Pass), soon heading towards Ponderosa and descending. Where the path bends right, pass to the left of the reedy area ahead, then follow a path initially between banks of heather and bilberry to rejoin your outward track.

WALK 13
CYRN-Y-BRAIN

DESCRIPTION A 4½ mile walk exploring the little known heather and bracken southern slopes of Cyrn-y-Brain, now an Open Access area, on delightful paths offering panoramic views. Allow about 3 hours.
START As **Walk 12**.

1 Follow instructions in paragraph **1** of **Walk 12**.

2 Take the right fork towards the near-by transmitter station, then turn RIGHT along a wide stony path past the station – *enjoying panoramic views.* The path soon bends towards Esclusham Mountain, then Ruabon Mountain and narrows. Later it continues across the moorland towards Craig y Forwyn at World's End – *with a good view down Eglwyseg Glen* – later descending to a path junction at a fence. Here turn RIGHT and follow the narrower path beside the fence, then across the steep hillside towards Llantisilio Mountain, with Fron-lwyd below. Later it steadily descends to cross a stream in a side valley. The path continues up the slope ahead

then crosses bracken/gorse/bilberry covered terrain, shortly descending to cross streams. Soon the path widens and continues to reach a gap in a small ridge.

3 Here turn RIGHT and follow a wide path passing behind the small ridge – *a good place to stop.* The delightful green path climbs steadily past a path on the right, shortly with a good view down into the old Horseshoe Pass. Later when it splits continue up the left fork. After levelling out it crosses the top of a steep side valley – *with a view of the Ponderosa* – then descends to a fence corner. The path continues briefly beside the fence before angling away to join your outward track. As you approach a brick and concrete structure – *apparently the base of a World War II radar mast* – take a path angling LEFT and follow it near the fence to a stile. Keep ahead to cross the road, then the Ponderosa's southern car park to the start. The café makes a good finish to the walk

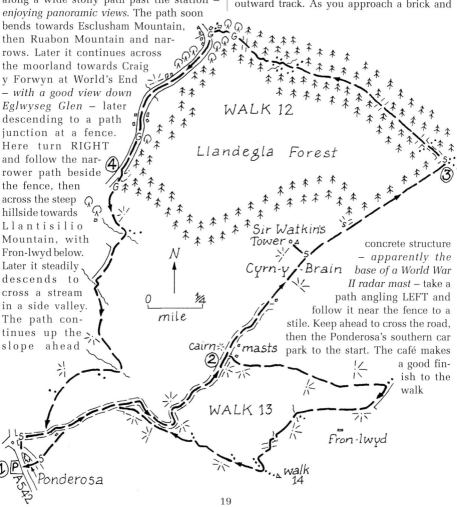

WALK 12

Llandegla Forest

Sir Watkin's Tower

Cyrn-y-Brain

N

0   ¼
mile

cairn   masts

WALK 13

Fron-lwyd

walk 14

Ponderosa
A542

WORLD'S END

DESCRIPTION An exhilarating 9 mile walk of great variety on good upland paths and tracks, with panoramic views. The route crosses heather moorland and upland pasture on a long steady descent into Eglwyseg valley. It follows the valley road to World's End, where a path rises beneath Craig y Forwyn onto the moorland edge of Eglwyseg Mountain. After following Offa's Dyke Path to Llandegla Forest, the route crosses heather covered Cyrn-y-Brain (1847 feet/563 metres), with its ruin of Sir Watkin's Tower and transmitter masts, for a final descent on a stony access track. Allow about 5½ hours.

START Ponderosa Café & Gift Shop, Horseshoe Pass [SJ 193481]

DIRECTIONS See **Walk 12**

1 Cross the road to the Ponderosa and turn LEFT along the grass verge past the car park. At its corner, angle RIGHT across the side road and follow a path ahead through heather and gorse to a stile/gate on a stony track. Go along the track, then at old metal gateposts turn LEFT up the slope for a few yards. Just before an old metal fence post take a path angling RIGHT and continue with it through banks of heather. Go past the top end of a reedy area to join the bend of a clear path beyond. Follow the path up the slope ahead. At a slate waymark post take the right fork (Faraway). Later take its left fork to rejoin the nearby track by a waymark post.

2 Take the waymarked path opposite up through heather, soon angling RIGHT to join another path. Follow it up the hillside beneath the track safety barrier. When it splits keep ahead to follow a delightful path across the top of a steep side valley, and on towards distant Eglwyseg escarpment. The wide path makes a long steady descent, later passing to the left of a small ridge, where you are joined by another wide green path angling in on the left.

3 Continue ahead down to another slate waymarker post and follow the path

ahead (Eglwyseg valley). Go past the nearby ruin and follow the fence to two stiles by sheepfolds. Continue ahead to a gate, then follow the green track past an old quarry. Just before it descends left, take the waymarked path angling RIGHT to descend between an old boundary and a fence. At the bottom bend RIGHT to cross a stile near a ruin. Here descend LEFT through bracken to a tree boundary below and follow it down to a stile. Go along the field edge to a gate onto a green track and follow it LEFT up above woodland to a stile/gate. Follow another track ahead down past two houses, then continue down the access track to a road. Turn LEFT and follow the attractive hedge-lined road along the valley beneath the impressive limestone escarpment, later climbing steadily towards Craig y Forwyn – *'Maiden's Rock' – so called after a young woman thwarted in love, threw herself from the summit.* After passing Offa's Dyke Path cross a stile ahead on the bend by the ford.

4 Follow the path up the wooded valley beneath the scree slopes of Craig y Forwyn to a rock face, where the stream disappears underground. Continue up the narrow wooded valley past cave entrances to cross a stile at the top. Follow the path angling up LEFT for about 10 yards, then turn RIGHT up a path to join a nearby narrow stony track. Follow it LEFT across the moorland past two waymarked side paths, then take either fork. Continue with the track, later becoming reedy in nature, to a road. Go along the road, soon rising and continuing across the expansive moorland.

5 At a slate waymarker post turn LEFT and follow the Offa's Dyke Path, partly boardwalked, through heather and bilberry. After about ¾ mile, at a row of sleeper supports, just before a ladder-stile/gate at the edge of Llandegla Forest, follow a clear narrow path heading through the heather parallel with the nearby forest perimeter. After the forest corner the path improves and climbs steadily with the fence. When it levels out a stile gives access to the trig point and the remains of Sir Watkin's Tower – *built as a folly by a prominent landowner on a Bronze Age cairn in the late 18thC or early 19thC.* Continue to the wireless station ahead, then follow its stony access track past further transmitter masts, after which the track begins a long steady meandering descent to the A452 by the Ponderosa.

1 - 2 Follow instructions in paragraphs 1-2 of **Walk 14**.

Craig y Forwyn

3 Turn sharp LEFT along this path and follow it across the bracken covered terrain. Later it becomes narrower, then descends to cross a stream in a hidden side valley. Follow the path ahead up and across the hillside, later alongside a fence to join a wider path. Keep ahead briefly alongside the fence, soon bending left then descending to cross a stream in a side valley. Continue up the stony path ahead and across the moorland, soon on a long steady descent past a side valley on the right into a shallow valley and up to join a minor road above. Turn LEFT along the road for ½ mile, then follow instructions in paragraph **5** of **Walk 14**.

WALK 15

CYRN-Y-BRAIN

DESCRIPTION A 7¼ mile walk exploring Cyrn-y-Brain, on delightful paths and tracks. The route follows Walk 14 across heather moorland and upland pasture, then crosses Cyrn-y-Brain's lesser known southern slopes, now Open Access land, before returning with Walk 14. Allow about 4½ hours.
START As **Walk 14**.

EGLWYSEG ESCARPMENT

DESCRIPTION An exhilarating 10 mile walk for experienced walkers exploring the dramatic limestone escarpment of Eglwyseg Mountain, offering panoramic views. From World's End the route follows a waymarked path along the top of the impressive escarpment, later descending to a scenic upland road. Here it joins the Offa's Dyke Path for a return, which includes a superb section of the National Trail crossing scree slopes beneath the escarpment. Allow about 6 hours.

START World's End car park [SJ232484] or from beneath Trevor Rocks [SJ234431]

DIRECTIONS The car park near the end of the forest is accessed by minor roads from the A542 just north of the Brittania Inn, or by minor moorland road from the B5426 near New Brighton. The alternative start is accessed by minor road from the Sun Trevor Inn on the A539.

*C*reigiau **Eglwyseg** and the adjoining Trevor Rocks extending south from World's End form one of the finest carboniferous limestone escarpments in Britain, nationally important for their extensive scree slopes and an Area of Special Scientific Interest. On the plateau above the escarpments are cairns, barrows, and kerb circles – evidence of Early Bronze Age occupation by man (2000–1300 BC).

I Turn LEFT up the road and just beyond the end of the trees go up a path on the right then turn RIGHT up a stony track. After about 20 yards, when it begins to bear left keep straight ahead along a stony path, parallel with another path and the track – *soon with good views down World's End across to Llantisilio Mountain and the Berwyns.* The path continues through bracken, briefly descending then rising to join a narrow stony track. Follow it RIGHT past a nearby waymarker post, soon bending past a fence corner. Keep with the main waymarked permissive path across the moorland – *with a view to Craig y Forwyn overlooking World's End.* At the fence corner the path bears LEFT across the bracken/heather hillside, soon along the top of a crag.

2 When it splits angle LEFT up the waymarked path – *with views to Llantisilio Mountain and Ponderosa – and on past Craig Arthur – with a good view of the Offa's Dyke Path crossing the scree slopes below.* Later the path descends to where a stream emerges and rises up the slope. It now continues away from the edge, following a small limestone escarpment across a heather/bracken/bilberry plateau, then bends down into another side valley – *a good place for a break.* Follow the waymarked path up beside the stream to reach a waymarked path junction after about 150 yards.

3 Turn RIGHT across the stream and follow the path up to a small metal gate in a fence – *enjoying new views west to Arenig and down the valley to Llangollen, and distant Shropshire Hills.* Continue with the path – *enjoying views west along the wooded Dee valley and east to the heather covered Ruabon Mountain, then Castell Dinas Bran towering above Llangollen* – later descending to a signposted path junction. Follow the permissive path ahead across a limestone area with small trees, then alongside a fence on your left on a steady descent, after which continue down the hillside to a minor road.

4 Turn RIGHT – *you are now on the Offa's Dyke Path* – soon passing the alternative start. Continue along this delightful upland road, appropriately named the Panorama Walk, beneath impressive Trevor Rocks and towards Castell Dinas Bran. At two junctions keep ahead, after which the road bends north west beneath the limestone escarpment. Later the Offa's Dyke Path leaves the road and goes up an access track to a house, then continues north across scree slopes beneath your outward route to eventually reach the minor road at World's End. Follow it across the ford and up to the car park.

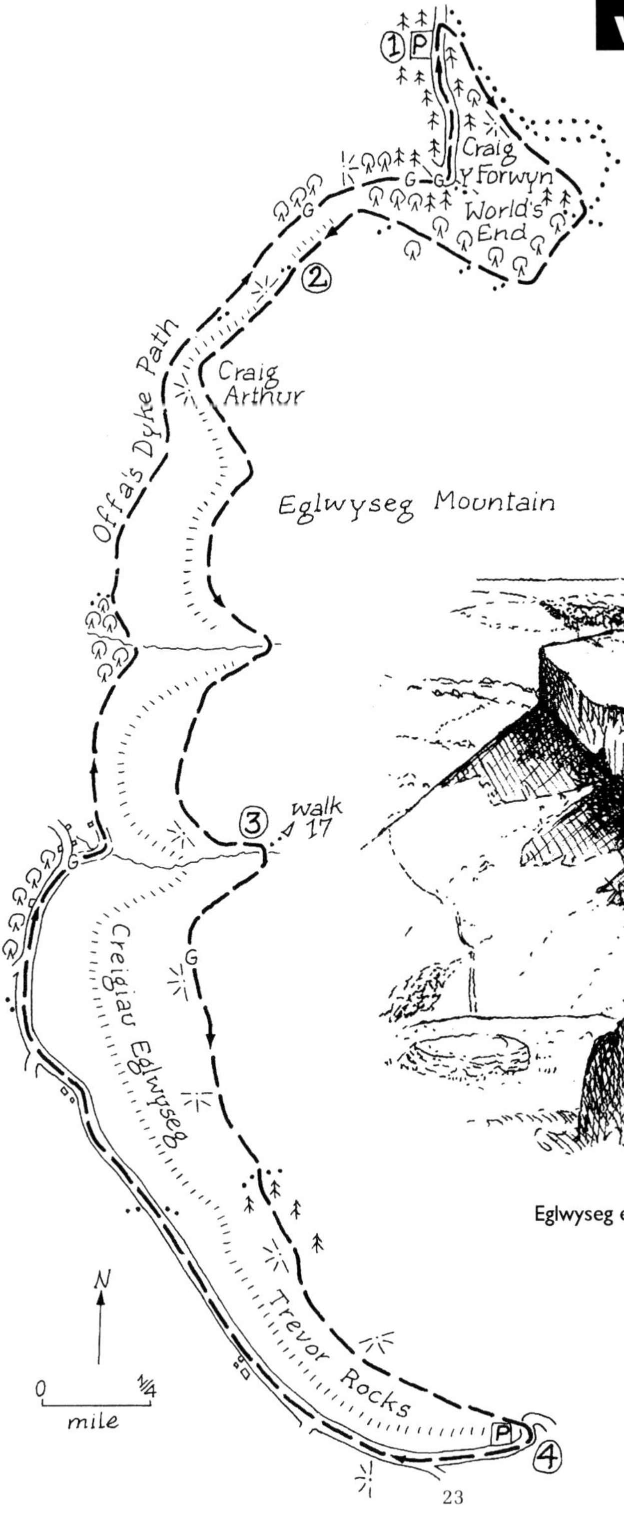

① P

Craig
y Forwyn

G—G

World's
End

②

Offa's Dyke Path

Craig
Arthur

Eglwyseg Mountain

③ walk
17

Creigiau Eglwyseg

G

N

Trevor Rocks

P ④

0 ¼
mile

Eglwyseg escarpment

WALK 17

EGLWYSEG & RUABON MOUNTAINS

DESCRIPTION A challenging 9½ mile walk for experienced walkers featuring contrasting limestone escarpment and heather moorland. The route follows a waymarked path along the dramatic limestone edges of Eglwyseg Mountain before heading east across the expansive heather moorland of Ruabon Mountain to descend to Newtown Mountain Forest. After skirting the moorland edge it returns on a good path across Ruabon Mountain.

START World's End car park [SJ232484]
DIRECTIONS See **Walk 16**.

*R*uabon Mountain, *where lead was once mined, was bought by Sir Watkin Williams Wynn from the Crown in 1857, and his gamekeepers managed the heather moor for grouse shooting, which became one of the most prolific in Wales. In recent years, as grouse numbers have greatly reduced, action has been taken to improve moorland management, and help sustain the rare black grouse. The famous 19thC travel writer George Borrow crossed the moor from World's End en route to Wrexham. In August 1940 the mountain burned from bombs dropped by German planes, heading to and from Liverpool.*

1-2 Follow instructions in paragraphs **1-2** of **Walk 16**.

3 Follow the wide path ahead up through bracken, passing a line of limestone to a cross path. Follow the narrow path ahead through bracken. After about 60 yards turn RIGHT and follow a clear path across heather covered Ruabon Mountain – *enjoying extensive views to the Shropshire Hills, and later across Cheshire to the Pennines. The path then begins a long steady descent – with views from Wrexham extending north to Merseyside.* Later, after a cross path,

angle LEFT to pass through gorse to cross a gate in the wall ahead at Frozen Clock. *During the 19thC brooms were manufactured from heather in the ruined building here. Apparently its name reflects the coldness of the location which caused the works clock to stop!* Keep ahead then go along a green track, soon bearing LEFT across a stream. Turn

RIGHT down the field edge near the stream to a stile. The path continues along the left bank of the stream passing between mature and young conifers, to a footbridge over a stream – *a good place for a break.*

4 Keep ahead, then turn LEFT up a stony path through the wood to a stile/ gate into Open Access land. Turn RIGHT up a

5 Here turn LEFT along a track to a nearby kissing gate/gate into Open Access land. Angle LEFT up the waymarked path. At the fence corner keep ahead on the waymarked path up across the bracken/bilberry slope, over a green track leading to nearby Mountain Lodge. After crossing a wet area in a dip the clear path begins a long steady climb west across the heather/bracken cov-

cross

Mountain Lodge

Pant-glas reservoir

walk 18

walk 18

Ruabon Mountain

Newtown Mountain Forest

Frozen Clock

path through bracken to join a green track coming in from the left. Follow the old reedy track ahead near the perimeter fence of Newtown Mountain Forest. The track then continues across the moorland, later bending right to join a bridleway which you follow to a road. Follow it LEFT past Pant Glas reservoir – *built in 1941* – and a track on your left. After crossing a stream the road rises and bends right.

ered Ruabon Mountain, eventually levelling out and passing a cross of stones on the ground – *apparently a memorial to a crashed aircraft.* At the crossroad of paths beyond take the right fork ahead. Follow the path down through heather and across reedy terrain, then through bracken to a waymarked path junction. Continue ahead along a green track, soon taking either fork, to join your outward route.

WALK 18

NEWTOWN MOUNTAIN FOREST

DESCRIPTION A 6¼ mile (**A**) or 5¾ mile (**B**) walk exploring the countryside west of Rhos. The route heads south to Penycae then west past a reservoir to follow a bridleway through Newtown Mountain Forest and the edge of Ruabon Mountain. It then follows a choice of routes to Tai-nant before returning by field paths. Allow about 3½ hours. An alternative 4 mile walk (**C**) is included.

START Bethlehem Chapel, Rhos [SJ 289468]

DIRECTIONS Entering Rhos on the B5097 from the north go past Ysgol y Grango and just past the Coach & Horses pub turn right along Mountain Street. At the junction by the Sun Inn, turn left along Hall Street to find a lay-by by Llys-y-Mynydd and opposite Bethlehem Chapel.

Rhosllanerchrugog (known as 'Rhos') is a former coal mining village with a strong Welsh culture and language. It is famous for its male voice choirs which grew from the choral influence of its many nonconformist chapels. Nearby Hafod colliery (1863-1968) employed at its peak almost 2000 men.

I Continue along Hall Street then turn right along School Street to its end where it becomes a track. At the last house, Llys Maelor, go along a green track ahead to a gate. Continue up the track between fences, over a stream and on to go through a gate. Cross the stile on your left and continue along the edge of the adjoining field to a kissing gate, then turn RIGHT along a hedge-lined stony path. Later, keep ahead along a track, then take its right fork. When the track bends left at the rear of houses, turn RIGHT along an enclosed path to a stile/gate into a field. Follow the tree boundary on your left. At its end bear LEFT to a stile/gate, then follow the enclosed path to join a rough access lane, which descends to Poplar Road in Penycae.

2 Turn RIGHT and pass behind the bus shelter then go along Mill Lane. At The Granary continue ahead on the signposted path past cottages, through a small gate to a stile at the end of the last cottage, Nant-y-Felin. Follow the path through the wooded valley to the road. Follow it LEFT. On the bend just before Pentre farm turn RIGHT along a hedge-lined sunken multi-user path. *Known as Dark Lane, it was part of the ancient road from Ruabon to Llandegla.* (For **Walk C** follow the old way to a road. Follow it right to a junction by Mount View at Tai-nant. Go down the right fork and resume text at the second sentence in paragraph **5**.) After a few yards take a higher path on the left to a stile into a field. Continue alongside the hedge then at a gate in it follow a path leading half-LEFT across the field to a stile in the hedge ahead. Follow the stiled path across several fields to a road. Turn RIGHT up the road.

3 Just beyond a house take the no through road on the left. Follow it past Gelli Wen and Orrillia, soon afterwards descending to a gate. Now follow a track past Top Reservoir – *built in 1902 to complement an earlier lower reservoir* – to gates into Newtown Mountain Forest. *Newtown village once stood here but it was abandoned and subsequently bought by the Water Company which used stone from its houses to build the reservoir. Follow the track through the forest.* About 40 yards after passing a wall on your left leading down to the stream take a stony bridleway on the right up through the trees, then north along the forest edge to enter Open Access land. Follow the bridleway along the bracken covered valley, soon rising.

4 Where it meets a wide path coming in from the right beneath a wall you have a choice. (For **Walk B** turn RIGHT and follow the path to a gate. Go along a green track to a nearby lane. Turn LEFT on the signposted path down an access lane. At the bottom turn LEFT to a gate at the left hand end of the building ahead. Turn RIGHT behind it and descend to cross a stile in a fence. Follow the fence on your right down the field, then the tree boundary on your left down to cross

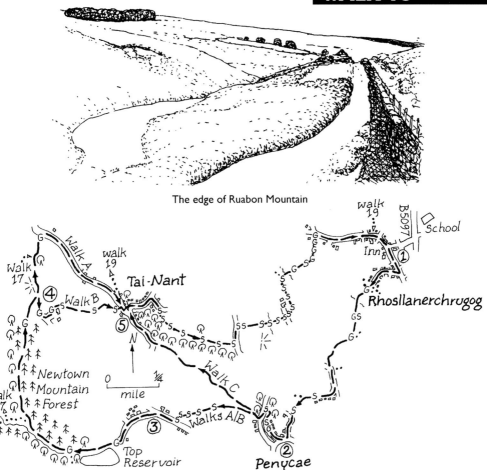

The edge of Ruabon Mountain

a stile in the field corner. Go across the field to the boundary ahead, then follow it RIGHT to a stile/gate by the Old Chapel House onto the road at Tai-nant. Turn RIGHT to point **5**.) For **Walk A** turn LEFT and continue with the bridleway along the rim of the valley and on to a road. Turn RIGHT and follow this quiet country road for ½ mile to pass the Old Chapel House in Tai-Nant.

5 Take a railed path on the left down to a telephone box onto the road below. Cross the stone bridge over the stream and follow the road past houses, then turn RIGHT along the no through road. On the bend cross an iron stile by a gate ahead and follow the green track to another stile/gate. Now fol-

low the stiled path through five fields to a road. Follow it LEFT then cross a stile on the right. Follow the stiled path through several further fields to reach an access track to a nearby farm. Cross the iron stile opposite and go along the field edge to another iron stile. Turn LEFT along the next field edge to a stile/gate by the farmhouse. Go along the hedge-lined green track to an iron stile/gate. Follow the hedge on your right to a stile/gate, then a narrow path to cross a footbridge over a stream. Go across the field to a kissing gate by a telegraph pole, then angle LEFT to a stile and on to a nearby kissing gate. Continue through three further kissing gates to a road. Follow it RIGHT past Coppi Industrial estate to the start.

WALK 19
CAE-LLWYD & TY MAWR RESERVOIRS

DESCRIPTION A varied 7 mile (**A**) or 5 mile (**B**) walk featuring two upland 19thC reservoirs. The route first goes to the attractive remote hamlet of Tai-nant then heads north to Cae-llwyd reservoir. Walk A does a circular extension north to Fron-deg, returning across the moorland edge of Ruabon Mountain. After passing Ty Mawr reservoir the route returns by quiet roads, field and woodland paths. Allow about 4 hours.

START Bethlehem Chapel, Rhos [SJ 289468]

DIRECTIONS See **Walk 18**.

*T*o the north west *of Rhos are two large reservoirs built to collect water from the adjoining moorland of Ruabon Mountain to meet the increasing demand for water in Wrexham and elsewhere. Cae-llwyd reservoir was completed in 1878 and Ty Mawr was opened with great ceremony in 1907.*

1 Follow Hall Street past the Sun Inn and Llyn Einion Road. You pass Park Lodge. *On its front is a stone sun emblem – part of the crest of the Jones family, Llancrchrugog estate owners in the 18thC.* After passing Coppi Industrial estate – *the site of a former brickworks* – continue up Hall Lane past the ornate entrance to Cai Einion Farm. Soon go through a kissing gate on the left. After two further kissing gates go along the field edge to another. At a stile ahead angle RIGHT across the field to a kissing gate by a telegraph pole and on to a footbridge over a stream. Follow the path to a stile then turn RIGHT along the field edge to another stile. Go up the next field to cross a stile below Ty Canol. Turn RIGHT to another stile and follow the enclosed path round to the entrance. Turn LEFT along the road. Shortly, cross a stile on the right and go along the field to an iron barred stile in the tree boundary ahead. Go along the edge of the next three fields to

Bryn Celyn, then follow the lane past other cottages to a T junction.

2 Turn LEFT down the road and through the hamlet of Tai-nant. After crossing a small stone bridge over the stream take a railed path from behind the telephone box up to another road. Follow it RIGHT past the Old Chapel House and a cottage. At The Larches take a signposted path down an access track and over the stream to Laburnum Cottage. Go through a large gate at its end and follow a path through bracken, soon bending right and climbing the steep slope ahead to a stile. Go up the large field to a hedge/fence corner on the skyline ahead to cross a waymarked iron fence section just beyond – *offering extensive views.* Go across the field and through a gateway ahead, then continue along the edge of the next two fields to a road. Turn LEFT and cross a stile on the right. Go across the large field to join a track. When it bends left cross a stile in the tree boundary ahead. Go across the large field – *soon with a view of Cae-llwyd reservoir ahead* – then along the field edge past the right hand side of the reservoir – *soon looking down to Ty Mawr reservoir.* After passing the end of the reservoir go down the thistle-covered slope below to join an old iron fence. Continue on its other side and at its end keep ahead to a stile onto a track junction. (For **Walk B** go along the track ahead and resume text at paragraph **5**.)

3 Turn LEFT down the track to cross the reservoir's outflow. Just beyond the gate at a finger post turn RIGHT up a farm track, then continue ahead across the field to descend to a small bridge. Cross a sleeper bridge to its left and a stile then go up the slope. Follow the fence on your left, soon passing along a grass shelf, to a stile/gate above 17thC Plas-yn-fron. Follow its driveway to a road junction and go up the road ahead, then cross a stile on the left. Follow the boundary on your right, soon passing woodland. At a gate in the boundary bear RIGHT with the path towards a transmitter mast. Just before a stile by the substation turn sharp LEFT on a path beside the tree boundary.

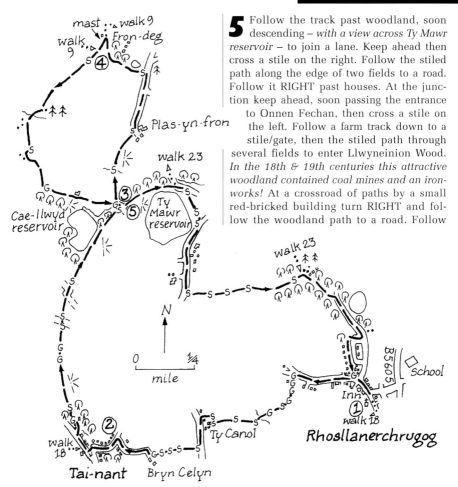

5 Follow the track past woodland, soon descending – *with a view across Ty Mawr reservoir* – to join a lane. Keep ahead then cross a stile on the right. Follow the stiled path along the edge of two fields to a road. Follow it RIGHT past houses. At the junction keep ahead, soon passing the entrance to Onnen Fechan, then cross a stile on the left. Follow a farm track down to a stile/gate, then the stiled path through several fields to enter Llwyneinion Wood. *In the 18th & 19th centuries this attractive woodland contained coal mines and an ironworks!* At a crossroad of paths by a small red-bricked building turn RIGHT and follow the woodland path to a road. Follow

4 At the fence corner, as the path bends right, keep ahead across reedy/gorse terrain to cross a stile. Follow a path through reeds and bracken parallel with the nearby boundary, later joining it. At a small plantation go past a stile then angle RIGHT to cross a stream. Continue ahead, then at a path junction, follow a path LEFT through reeds and bracken to cross a long stile over a wall. Turn RIGHT and just before the boundary corner turn LEFT along a path through bracken to join a green track. Follow it down to a gateway, then above a small wooded valley, past a ruin and on down to join your outward route to reach the track junction at point **3**. Turn LEFT.

it RIGHT – *with a glimpse of a lake below on the site of a former Tile and Brickworks (1883-1929)* – then take the first road on the right. From the top corner of the parking area follow a path through trees ahead, then LEFT along the former Wrexham-Rhos railway line (1901-63) to Hall Street.

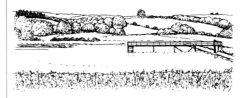

Cae-llwyd reservoir

WALK 20

NANT MILL (I)

DESCRIPTION A delightful 2½ mile walk following the first part of the waymarked Clywedog Valley Trail to Nant Mill Visitor Centre, returning along the other side of the wooded valley. Allow about 2 hours.

START Minera Lead Mines Centre [SJ 276509]

DIRECTIONS See **Walk 8**.

*M*inera – meaning 'ore' in Latin – has been associated with lead mining probably since the Roman times, but the first known record is 1296. Piecemeal surface mining continued for centuries afterwards, then in the 18thC large scale deep mining began to exploit the area's mineral wealth, including zinc and silver. Flooding was a problem which was initially tackled by the digging of drainage channels. The deepest, dug in 1847, aptly named Deep Day, emerges near Nant Mill. From the late 18thC steam engines were used to pump water out of the mines. Fortunes fluctuated during the 19thC, but by its end the industry was faced with increased costs, falling ore prices and declining reserves, and by 1914 mining had ceased.

The Lead Mines Centre is on the site of the deepest shaft (1220 feet), whose restored beam engine house, of Cornish design, pumped water from the mine from 1857 until 1907. Nearby are the remains of lead processing areas. Minera's development is also associated with limestone quarrying to the west.

I From the car park follow the pathway up to a finger post by the nearby Visitor Centre. Turn LEFT along the signposted Clywedog Trail to a kissing gate to reach the road. Cross it and walk along the grass verge to take the signposted Nant Mill path along a track past a house. After two stiles follow the green track to another stile, then go along the fenced path past fields – *reputedly part of a tramway for transporting limestone to*

Bersham Ironworks – then down the edge of a wooded valley to a stile. *In the wood are early coal workings, known as bellpits.* Angle LEFT to a waymarked gap by a footbridge over the river above a ford. Follow the path near the river along the wooded valley, shortly passing above a deep wooded gorge. At the end of a clearing there is a choice of waymarked trail paths to Nant Mill. One branch descends to a footbridge over the river by the Deep Day drainage level and continues along its opposite bank. The other continues along the right bank to a gate and information board, then descends a narrow road to cross a footbridge over the river above the ford, to enter the car park.

Nant Mill

2 Immediately beyond the Visitor Centre, turn LEFT to follow a path past its side up through the trees to the road. Follow it up to the junction, then turn LEFT along the shady road signposted to Nant. Shortly go down Heol Penyfelin to reach the footbridge and ford met on your outward route. Take a path signposted to Pant Tywyll along the access track ahead, then behind the house to a stile. Follow the enclosed stiled path beneath a wooded slope to reach a tarmaced path junction below Coedpoeth. Turn LEFT down the handrailed path, past a side path, to cross a footbridge over the river. Follow the enclosed path up to the road opposite the entrance to the Lead Mines Centre.

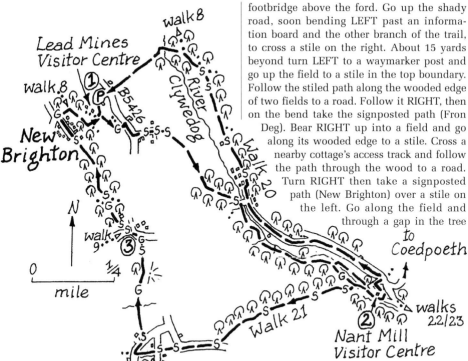

footbridge above the ford. Go up the shady road, soon bending LEFT past an information board and the other branch of the trail, to cross a stile on the right. About 15 yards beyond turn LEFT to a waymarker post and go up the field to a stile in the top boundary. Follow the stiled path along the wooded edge of two fields to a road. Follow it RIGHT, then on the bend take the signposted path (Fron Deg). Bear RIGHT up into a field and go along its wooded edge to a stile. Cross a nearby cottage's access track and follow the path through the wood to a road. Turn RIGHT then take a signposted path (New Brighton) over a stile on the left. Go along the field and through a gap in the tree boundary ahead by a stream. Go through the next field and the gate ahead. Continue along the next field edge – *enjoying good views towards Shropshire, Cheshire and distant Pennines* – to a waymarked gateway in the corner. Follow the path ahead, soon through an avenue of trees, to a stile, then go through the gate opposite onto a road. Follow it LEFT.

WALK 21

NANT MILL (2)

DESCRIPTION A 3 mile walk following the first part of the waymarked Clywedog Valley Trail to Nant Mill Visitor Centre, returning by higher field paths. Allow about 2 hours.
START Minera Lead Mines Centre [SJ 276509]
DIRECTIONS See **Walk 8**.

*N*ant Mill Visitor Centre *is a former corn mill dating from 1832. It stands on the site of an earlier fulling mill used to clean and thicken woollen cloth, later becoming a corn mill.*

1 Follow instructions in paragraph **1** of **Walk 20**, taking the trail path along the opposite bank of the river in the final section to Nant Mill.

2 From the Visitor Centre head to the car park corner by the river to cross a

3 Take a signposted path (New Brighton) over a stile by a gated access drive. Go to another stile ahead, then follow a green track past the end of the house and through trees to a gate. Go to a stile/gate ahead, then follow the path through the wood to a stile/gate onto a road at New Brighton. Follow it past houses and a black corrugated Methodist church. Go through a kissing gate on the right by a Council noticeboard and telephone box to enter the Country Park. Descend steps and follow the path to a cross path by a seat amongst trees. Follow it RIGHT through the trees, then at a finger post at a path junction turn LEFT and follow the path down to the start of the Clywedog trail.

WALK 22

BERSHAM IRONWORKS

DESCRIPTION A 3 mile walk following the Clywedog Valley Trail through ancient woodland past a section of Offa's Dyke, to Bersham Ironworks (check opening times), then returning along the opposite side of the attractive wooded valley. Allow about 2 hours.

START Nant Mill Visitor Centre [SJ 289501]

DIRECTIONS At the eastern end of Coedpoeth take a minor road south from the A525 signposted to Nant Mill.

*B*ersham Ironworks *first established about 1718, developed under John Wilkinson's ownership during the late 18thC into one of Europe's most important, renowned for its steam-engines and cannon.*

From the Visitor Centre follow the access road east up to a junction. Go down the road to a kissing gate into Plas Power Woods – *part of an early 17thC estate and now owned by the Woodland Trust.* Follow the main path – *believed to be an 18thC tramway built to carry limestone from Minera to the Bersham Ironworks* – through the mature woodland and past Offa's Dyke earthwork. After diverting to an impressive weir – *built in the mid 19thC to supply water to a nearby coal mine* – continue through the wood to reach the more elegant Caeau weir – *used in the 18thC to provide water to the Bersham Ironworks.* Follow the old leat to the entrance to Bersham Ironworks car park. Continue alongside the leat, then descend to the road. Follow it to the Ironworks.

2 Return along the road past St Mary's – *a private estate church (1875)* – then Bersham Lodge, after which the road rises. Shortly, go through a kissing gate on the right. Follow the old green track through the wood to the weir passed earlier. Continue with the path

near the river, soon rising to a stile adjoining Offa's Dyke. Now follow a permissive path along the wooded field edge to a small gate, then across the mid-slopes to join the wooded boundary ahead. After a gate go along the bottom edge of the next long field, later rising to a stile to re-enter Plas Power Woods. Now follow a permissive bridleway down to the river and on through the wood to the road. Follow it RIGHT across Nant Bridge to return to Nant Mill.

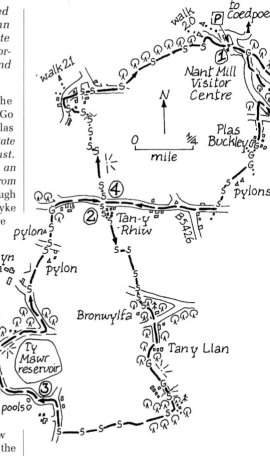

WALK 23

TY MAWR RESERVOIR

DESCRIPTION A 6½ mile figure of eight walk (**A**) exploring the attractive varied countryside south of the Clywedog valley. Allow about 4 hours. A shorter 3 mile walk (**B**) is included.
START Nant Mill Visitor Centre [SJ 289501]
DIRECTIONS See **Walk 22**.

I From the Centre follow the access road east up to a junction. Go down the road and across Nant bridge, then follow a permissive bridleway through Plas Power Woods, shortly rising away from the river and continuing up the wood edge to a road. Follow it RIGHT then take a signposted path on the left through more woodland to another road. Go

along the drive opposite to Plas Buckley. Go past the house and through farm buildings to a waymarked gate. Go along the track to another gate. After about 50 yards further go through a waymarked gate on the right. Angle LEFT up the long field past pylons to cross two stiles in the tree boundary and continue to a stile onto a road. Follow it RIGHT to the T junction. Turn RIGHT along the B5426, then take a minor road on the left and follow it up past a farm to Tan-y-Rhiw. (For **Walk B** cross a stile on the right and continue from paragraph **4**.)

2 Take a signposted stiled path on the left past buildings, then through several fields to a road. Cross the stile opposite, then go across the field and down to a stile into a wood. Follow the path to a footbridge then through the lower gardens of Bronwylfa to the road. Turn RIGHT then LEFT along Tan y Llan's access lane. At the 16thC house continue on a path along the wood edge to a kissing gate. Go along the field edge to another kissing gate, then down a bungalow's access track. After crossing the stream, go over a stile ahead. Follow the path through the wood. At a crossroad of paths by a small building, follow a path RIGHT to a stile/gate. Now follow a stiled path west through several fields to a road. Follow it RIGHT.

3 At a junction turn LEFT along a lane. After a bungalow it becomes a track which rises steadily to a track junction. Turn RIGHT past woodland, soon descending – *with a view across Ty Mawr reservoir (1907)* – to a lane. Here do a sharp U – turn along Plas yn ffron farm's driveway. As it bends towards the farm cross a stile ahead. Go across the field, past a fence corner, then angle RIGHT to a gap in the hedge and on across the next field to a road. Turn RIGHT then LEFT over a nearby stile. Go up the field edge to a stile, then along the next two fields to a road. Follow it RIGHT down past a farm to Tan-y-Rhiw and cross a stile on the left.

4 Go across the field to a stile and across the next to a gateway in the hedge. Follow the tree boundary to cross a stile and another nearby. Follow the stiled path along the edge of the next two fields, then turn LEFT across a stream and on to a stile ahead. Go up the field edge and at the top, bear RIGHT then LEFT to a stile onto a road. Follow it RIGHT past two houses, then take a signposted path (Nant Mill) on the right. Follow it through the small wood, across an access track and on along the field edge. In the corner descend to the stream to reach the nearby road. Go down the road, then follow a stiled path along the wooded edge of two large fields. Descend the next field to a gap in the bottom tree boundary by a waymarker post, then turn RIGHT to a stile onto a narrow road. Follow it down to cross a footbridge over the river above the ford into Nant Mill's car park.

BERSHAM & FELIN PULESTON

2 Go through the car park, past a cottage and information board and follow the path ahead to cross a footbridge over the river into Puleston industrial estate. Go up the road to the A5152 and take the sign-posted path opposite to go through a metal gate at the end of Booker Cash and Carry. Go past the side of the building, through another gate, then follow the path through the trees to a stile. Heed the warning signs

DESCRIPTION A 2½ mile walk following a section of the Clywedog Valley Trail from Bersham Heritage Centre to Felin Puleston, returning by paths, road and a delightful bridle-way. Allow about 2 hours.

START Bersham Heritage Centre [SJ 312491]

DIRECTIONS The Centre is on the B5099 just east of the A483 Wrexham bypass and is well signposted.

*B*ersham *Heritage Centre, is housed in the former Bersham School (1876-1961), which stands on the site of Wilkinson's East Ironworks. It tells the story of John Wilkinson and his ironworks, plus other exhibitions. Open from Easter to the end of October – free admission. After ironmaking at Bersham declined at the beginning of the 19thC and moved to nearby Brymbo, water-powered papermaking became the prime activity in the valley.*

I Go along the roadside edge of the car park past a children's play area then angle RIGHT to descend a stepped path in the corner. At the bottom turn LEFT to join a road. Follow it ahead past houses then continue along a stony track, shortly crossing a bridge over the river. Now follow the waymarked trail along the riverbank to a stile. Continue briefly above the river, then go along the wooded right hand edge of the long field to a stile onto a lane. Follow it LEFT to cross a footbridge over the river. Turn RIGHT through a metal barrier, then take the path's right fork through the conservation area to cross a footbridge over the river. Follow the path under the railway and road bridges, then up through trees and down to Felin Puleston.

before crossing the railway line and a stile opposite. Follow the path to a road. Follow it LEFT past estate roads, then turn RIGHT along Homestead Lane. Later take a sign-posted mature tree-lined bridleway on the left. After ½ mile turn LEFT along a hedge-lined path to pass behind a cottage. Continue along its access track then cross a stile ahead on the bend. Go along the field edge, then after about 15 yards join a wall set back on the left. Follow the path alongside the wall through trees past a large house to a stile and on to join a lane which descends to the road. Follow it RIGHT to the start.

WALK 25

FELIN PULESTON & KING'S MILL

DESCRIPTION A 3¾ mile walk (**A**) following the final section of the Clywedog Valley Trail through attractive woodland to King's Mill, a former 14thC corn mill, returning near the river through Erddig Country Park. Allow about 2½ hours. Included are shorter 3¼ mile (**B**) and 2 mile (**C**) walks.

START Felin Puleston car park, Wrexham [SJ 325492]

DIRECTIONS Turn off the A5152 Wrexham-Rhostyllen road on a side road signposted to Erddig. Almost immediately turn left signposted Felin Puleston Countryside Centre down a track to a parking area by farm buildings.

Coed-y-Glyn WALK 25
lake
River Clywedog
King's Mill
A525

*F*elin Puleston *was the site of a corn mill from the 16thC until the late 18thC when it became part of a tenant farm. Further down the river is King's Mill built in the 14thC to grind corn for Wrexham residents. It retained its monopoly as the principal mill for Wrexham for centuries and was rebuilt by Philip Yorke of Erddig in 1769. However, after the introduction of steam-driven mills in Wrexham in the late 19thC King's Mill's fortunes declined and it eventually closed in 1940.*

1 Go past a cottage to an information board by an outbuilding, then follow the path ahead to cross a footbridge over the river and go through a kissing gate on the right. Follow the stony path near the river, past the weir which once served the mill, and a footbridge, and through kissing gates to eventually reach a lane/track – *with a view ahead to the lake.* Go through the kissing gate opposite and continue with the main path through the mature woodland of Coed-y-Glyn to a kissing gate onto a road. (For **Walk C** join the return route at the nearby car park.)

2 Go through the kissing gate opposite and continue with the woodland path. At a path junction keep ahead, then shortly take the right fork down to a stile into a field. Turn LEFT along the field edge, over a stream and on through a gateway to reach a kissing gate set back on the left. (For **Walk B** bear right down to a footbridge at point **3**.) Continue ahead along the wooded field edge and through a gap in the boundary. Later head down to a kissing gate/ information board by the river and follow the riverside path under the low road bridge to reach the restored King's Mill and a domed beehive kiln used in a nearby brickworks. Return under the road bridge and follow the riverside path to a kissing gate/gate, then the field edge round to a footbridge over the river.

3 Do not cross it but follow a field path ahead as shown, later rejoining the river. Continue along the riverbank, then across a field to a gate onto a road. Follow it RIGHT to enter a car park near your outward route and go through a kissing gate. Follow the path, soon beside an old leat to where it joins the river by a weir. Continue beside the shallow river, past the hidden lake, to eventually reach a track. Turn LEFT across the bridge over the river, then turn RIGHT and follow a wide stony path through kissing gates to reach the cottage near the start.

WALK 26

ERDDIG

DESCRIPTION A 4¾ mile **(A)** or 4 mile **(B)** walk around Erddig Country Park, perhaps combined with a visit to the house and gardens. The route follows the river east through attractive parkland. The return includes woodland paths, a late 11thC motte and bailey castle, Wat's Dyke, a classic view of Erddig, and interesting estate features. Allow about 3 hours.

START Felin Puleston car park, Wrexham [SJ 325492]

DIRECTIONS See **Walk 25**, or **Walk 27** for an alternative start from Erddig.

*E*rddig *was once one of the most important estates in North Wales. Its magnificent house dating from 1683, its gardens and parkland were owned by the Yorke family from the 18th until 1973 when they were left to the National Trust. The fascinating house, damaged by subsidence caused by coalmining, has been restored, and along with its parkland, now managed as a Country Park, attract thousands of visitors each year.*

1 Go past a nearby cottage and through a kissing gate by an information board. Follow the path past a footbridge and on through two kissing gates to reach a track. Turn LEFT across the nearby stone bridge, then go through a kissing gate on the right and follow a path beside the river. Later, after passing a hidden lake you cross the start of a leat by a weir. The path continues near the leat, crosses it, then heads to a small car park. At the road beyond turn RIGHT. Shortly go through a gate on the left. Follow the path across the meadow to briefly join the river then continue along the wooded field edge to a kissing gate. Go past a stile, cross a stream and through a gateway ahead. At a kissing gate to your left, follow a path leading RIGHT down to cross a footbridge over the river.

2 Follow the waymarked National Trust path up through trees above the river. The path continues through mature wood-

land, later descending to cross a footbridge over a stream and a stile beyond. Keep ahead to emerge into a field. Walk up the field to a waymarker post and continue up to a stile in the left hand corner onto a road. Follow it LEFT to a kissing gate on the right. Follow the wide path through the trees, past a waymarked side path, then along the wood edge. At a waymarker T-junction turn RIGHT and follow the path through the woodland – *once laid out as pleasure grounds with formal walks* – soon bending left and descending to a waymarker post. Go down to an information board below at the site of Erddig Motte and Bailey castle. Return to the main path and continue through the wood edge containing the earthen bank of Wat's Dyke to a T-junction. (For **Walk B** turn right and follow the path down to the track at point **4**.) Turn LEFT along the wide path near the walled garden, shortly bending RIGHT to reach the early 18thC ironwork gate and screen allowing a splendid view towards the house. Follow the path/track round to join the road at the car park exit.

3 Go along the road past the octagonal brick dovecote (1739). At crossroads keep ahead, then at a T junction turn RIGHT signposted to the 'Cup and Saucer.' At the former main entrance to the house turn LEFT down the lane and continue to a cattle grid/kissing gate, where it becomes a stony track. Just beyond turn LEFT over a nearby bridge to an information board on the hydraulic ram. *Installed in 1899 it helped pump water up to storage tanks in the house's roof and now powers the garden fountains. Just beyond is the cascade known as the 'Cup and Saucer ' built in 1775 to prevent erosion.*

4 Continue along the stony track, over the river and on through the parkland to join your outward path. Recross the bridge then angle LEFT to a kissing gate at the wood edge. Follow the path near the river through two kissing gates, past a footbridge then a weir. Keep with the main left fork to another kissing gate. Turn LEFT across the bridge over the river back to the start.

WALK 27

WAT'S DYKE

DESCRIPTION A 2¾ mile walk in Erddig Country Park and adjoining countryside full of interest, featuring an impressive section of Wat's Dyke. It combines well with a visit to the house and gardens. Allow about 2 hours.

START Erddig car park [SJ 328481]

DIRECTIONS Erddig lies 2 miles south of Wrexham and is signposted from the A5152 Wrexham-Rhostyllen road or A525 Whitchurch road.

*W*at's Dyke *consisted of a 2 metre high bank, with V-shaped ditch to the west. The earthwork ran from Basingwerk, Holywell for 40 miles to Shropshire. Its purpose and exact date is uncertain, but may well pre-date 8thC Offa's Dyke.*

1 Leave the car park by its exit and follow instructions in paragraph **3** of **Walk 26** to the 'Cup and Saucer'. Go through a metal kissing gate beyond it into a small wood. Follow a path LEFT to a kissing gate, then angle LEFT across the field – *with a good view of the house* – to cross a gated footbridge over Black Brook. Follow a path RIGHT by the stream to a kissing gate. Continue to a gate by a wood ahead, then follow the track up to Erddig's access drive. Follow it RIGHT, then at a late 19thC lodge go along a railed green track on the left. *Known as Green Lane this former estate road was originally part of an old drovers road to Welshpool.* Follow it past wooden sculptures.

2 Just beyond a kissing gate/gate, where the track bends between two ponds, take a waymarked path on the right. Follow the delightful tree-lined path to a kissing gate/gate, then go along the road to Sontley Country Cottages. Cross a stile on the right then follow the stiled path through several fields alongside the boundary containing the remains of Wat's Dyke to Erddig's access drive by Bryn Golau. Follow the access drive back to the start.

37

WALK 28

SONTLEY

DESCRIPTION A 7¾ mile walk (**A**) through part of Erddig estate and attractive farmland of Sontley estate to the south, featuring an impressive section of Wat's Dyke (See Walk 27 for details). Allow about 4½ hours. An alternative 5 mile walk (**B**) is included. Sontley is a family name dating to the 16thC.
START Felin Puleston car park, Wrexham [SJ 325492]
DIRECTIONS See **Walk 25**.

I Go past a cottage and an information board to cross a footbridge over the river, then go through a kissing gate on the right. Follow the stony path near the river, past the weir which once served Felin Puleston mill, and a footbridge, and through kissing gates to eventually reach a lane/track. Turn RIGHT along the stony track, soon crossing the bridge over the river. Continue along the track, then soon after crossing another bridge, go across a footbridge on the right to an information board on the hydraulic ram. *Installed in 1899 it helped pump water up to storage tanks in the house's roof and now powers the garden fountains. Nearby is the cascade known as the 'Cup and Saucer ' built in 1775 to prevent erosion.* Go through a metal kissing gate beyond the 'Cup and Saucer' into a small wood. Follow a path LEFT to a kissing gate, then angle LEFT across the field – *with a good view of Erddig* – to cross a gated footbridge over Black Brook. Follow a path RIGHT by the stream to a kissing gate. Continue to a gate by a wood ahead, then follow the track up to Erddig's access drive. Follow it RIGHT to a late 19thC lodge. (For **Walk B** go along a railed green track on the left. *Known as Green Lane this former estate road was originally part of an old drovers road to Welshpool.* Follow it to a kissing gate/gate and between ponds, then cross a stile on the right. Go across two fields to a road. Turn left, then right at the junction to join returning Walk A at point **4**.)

2 Continue along the road, then cross an iron stile opposite Bryn Golau to join Wat's Dyke Way. Follow the stiled path through several fields alongside the boundary containing the remains of Wat's Dyke. At a road by Middle Sontley turn LEFT and cross a stile on the right. Follow a nearby farm track along the long field to cross a facing stile in the corner. Go along the next two fields, then follow a narrow path along the tree-lined top of Wat's Dyke to a road. Cross the stile opposite and follow the boundary to the field corner to cross a nearby stile on Wat's Dyke. The path continues briefly along the tree-topped earthwork, then follows the field edge to a stile/footbridge/stile. Go along the edge of the next two fields, then follow a hedge-lined farm track LEFT to a track junction by a house. Turn LEFT and follow the enclosed stony access track past Clwt to the road.

3 Take a signposted path along a track opposite to a gate by an old house. Go ahead across the field to a stile in the corner. Now follow the hedge on your right across the field to a stile, then angle LEFT across the next field to join the fence ahead by a small pool – *an old marl pit.* Follow the fence to a stile/gate in the corner. After another nearby stile/gate, go along the field edge to a gate in the corner. Descend to another gate onto a road by medieval Old Sontley Hall. Follow it LEFT past the extensive outbuildings of Old Sontley farm, later rising to pass Millfield House.

4 Turn RIGHT past the front of the Old Smithy, then descend the narrow stony track through the trees – *a medieval packhorse route* – past the remains of Old Sontley Mill and on to cross a large footbridge over the stream. Keep ahead then go through a waymarked small gate on the left. Turn LEFT, then after a few yards RIGHT up into a field corner. Bear LEFT along the field towards a distant telegraph pole. Just beyond a solitary tree to your right, turn RIGHT towards the farm and past a waymarked telegraph pole to join the hedge/tree boundary beyond. Follow it LEFT to a stile in the corner. Go up the field then down to a stile/footbridge. Go

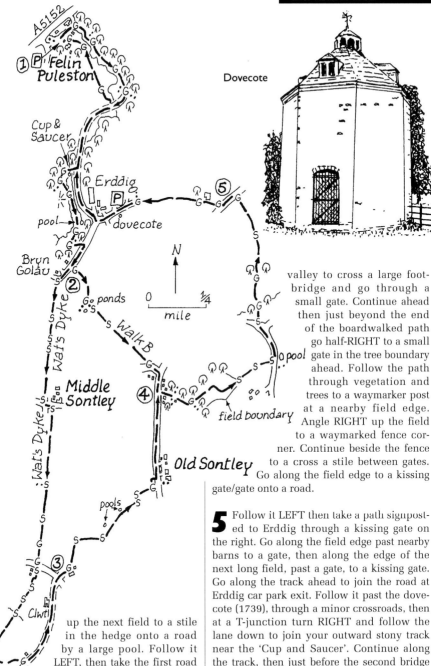

Dovecote

valley to cross a large foot-bridge and go through a small gate. Continue ahead then just beyond the end of the boardwalked path go half-RIGHT to a small gate in the tree boundary ahead. Follow the path through vegetation and trees to a waymarker post at a nearby field edge. Angle RIGHT up the field to a waymarked fence corner. Continue beside the fence to a cross a stile between gates. Go along the field edge to a kissing gate/gate onto a road.

5 Follow it LEFT then take a path signpost-ed to Erddig through a kissing gate on the right. Go along the field edge past nearby barns to a gate, then along the edge of the next long field, past a gate, to a kissing gate. Go along the track ahead to join the road at Erddig car park exit. Follow it past the dove-cote (1739), through a minor crossroads, then at a T-junction turn RIGHT and follow the lane down to join your outward stony track near the 'Cup and Saucer'. Continue along the track, then just before the second bridge over the river, turn LEFT along a stony path. Follow it through kissing gates back to the cottage at the start.

up the next field to a stile in the hedge onto a road by a large pool. Follow it LEFT, then take the first road on the left to another. Cross the stile opposite and go slightly RIGHT across the field to descend into a small wooded

PRONUNCIATION

Welsh	English equivalent
c	always hard, as in **cat**
ch	as in the Scottish word lo**ch**
dd	as th in **then**
f	as f in o**f**
ff	as ff in o**ff**
g	always hard as in **got**
ll	no real equivalent. It is like 'th' in then, but with an 'L' sound added to it, giving 'thlan' for the pronunciation of the Welsh 'Llan'.

KEY TO THE MAPS

- ➼ Walk route and direction
- ═ Metalled road
- ─ ─ ─ Unsurfaced road
- • • • • Footpath/route adjoining walk route
- ⌇ River/stream
- ♣ ♧ Trees
- ▬▭▬ Railway
- **G** Gate
- **S** Stile
- F.B. Footbridge
- ☼ Viewpoint
- P Parking
- T Telephone

THE COUNTRYSIDE CODE

- Be safe – plan ahead and follow any signs
- Leave gates and property as you find them
- Protect plants and animals, and take your litter home
- Keep dogs under close control
- Consider other people

Open Access
Some routes cross areas of land where walkers have the legal right of access under The CRoW Act 2000 introduced in May 2005. Access can be subject to restrictions and closure for land management or safety reasons for up to 28 days a year. Please respect any notices. The Countryside Council for Wales website (www.ccw.gov.uk) provides updated information on any closures.

Please contact the local Highways Department regarding any path problems encountered
Walks 1– 6   Flintshire Highways Department 01352 701233/4
Walks 7–10, 17–28   Wrexham Highways Department 01978 292057
Walks 11–16   Denbighshire Highways Department 01824 706872

About the author, David Berry

David is an experienced walker with a love of the countryside and an interest in local history. He is the author of a series of walks guidebooks covering North Wales, where he has lived and worked for many years, as well as a freelance writer for Walking Wales magazine. He has worked as a Rights of Way surveyor across North Wales and served as a member of Denbighshire Local Access Forum.

Whether on a riverside ramble, mountain or long distance walk, he greatly appreciates the beauty, culture and history of the landscape and hopes that his comprehensive guidebooks will encourage people to explore on foot its diverse scenery and rich heritage.

Published by **Kittiwake-Books Limited**
3 Glantwymyn Village Workshops, Glantwymyn, Machynlleth, Montgomeryshire SY20 8LY
© Text & map research: David Berry 2010
www.davidberrywalks.co.uk
© Maps & illustrations: Kittiwake 2010
Drawings by Morag Perrott
Cover photos: Main – The eastern edge of Ruabon Mountain. *Inset* – Minera Lead Mines Centre. David Berry
Care has been taken to be accurate. However neither the author nor the publisher can accept responsibility for any errors which may appear, or their consequences. If you are in any doubt about access, check before you proceed.
Printed by Mixam UK.
ISBN: **978 1 902302 83 6**